Through Children's Minds: The Marketing and Creation of Children's Products

Through Children's Minds

Previous Books by Stanley Goldstein
www.drstanleygoldstein.com

Nonfiction
Troubled Children/Troubled Parents: The Way Out
2nd Edition

Shopping For a Shrink:
Finding the Right Psychotherapist
For You or Your Child

Mental Health in a Minute: One-Hundred and One,
One Minute Lessons to Improve Your Life

Fiction
Ghosts and Angels
Park West
Lies in Progress
The Unintended

Through Children's Minds

Stanley Goldstein, Ph.D.

Through Children's Minds: The Marketing and Creation Of Children's Products

Wyston Books, Inc.

Through Children's Minds

Wyston Books, Inc.
www.wystonbooks.com

Goldstein, Stanley
Through children's minds: the marketing and creation of children's products
1. Children's Products
2. Marketing
3. Advertising
4. Television

Library of Congress Control Number: 2013915382
ISBN (Print) 978-0-9855847-6-4
ISBN (E-Book) 978-0-9855847-7-1
Cover Photograph by Carmen MartA-nez BanAs/
E+ Collection/Licensed From Getty Images

BISAC: BUS00200 Advertising & Promotion
BUS070060 Media & Communications
BUS057000 Industries/Retailing
BUS043060 Marketing/Research
SOC047000 Children's Studies

Copyright © 2013 by Stanley Goldstein
All rights reserved
Printed in the United States of America

Through Children's Minds

To children, who dream of their future and can hardly wait until *then*...

Through Children's Minds

Contents

Author's Note...9

Foreword: Who Should Read This Book...11

Introduction: How the Marketing To Children Began...15

Chapter 1: What Children Are *Really* Like...21

Chapter 2: The Behavior of The Child As Customer...31

Chapter 3: The Psychology of The Child As Customer...35

Chapter 4: Why Children Buy...45

Chapter 5: How Child Customers Differ From Adult Customers...51

Chapter 6: Maturing From Child to Adult Customer...57

Chapter 7: The Child As Influencer of Family Purchases...59

Chapter 8: The Global Children's Market...67

Chapter 9: Developmental Changes in Play...73

Chapter 10: Child Psychology
And Children's Products...81

Chapter 11: The Art of Developing
Children's Products...89

Chapter 12: The Uniqueness of
Marketing to Children...99

Chapter 13: What You Must Know
To Create New Marketing Ideas...107

Chapter 14: Marketing to Children
Which Will Likely Fail...119

Chapter 15: Advertising to
The Youth Market...127

Chapter 16: How Children
Relate to Television...137

Chapter 17: What Makes Children's
Television Commercials Effective?...157

Chapter 18: Is Television Advertising
Still Critical In the Digital Age?...175

Chapter 19: Promotional Activities
With Children...181

Chapter 20: Marketing, Children's Orientating,
And Conducting Market Research...189

Through Children's Minds

Author's Note

My thought of writing *Through Children's Minds* originated in workshops on telecommunications and marketing which I prepared under the auspices of Behavioral Information Services. The telecommunications workshop explained eighty percent of the telecommunications section in the *Encyclopedia of Engineering* in just one day. My goal was comparable for the Children's Marketing Workshop.

This book requires no prior knowledge of advertising, marketing, or child psychology. Its only requirement is the willingness to abandon the inaccurate explanations of children's behavior which each person, naturally and intuitively, has created, the "naïve psychology" to which Fritz Heider, a leading figure in the field of social psychology, devoted a lifetime of study.

Discarding cherished conclusions is difficult for these are the bedrock of our personality. Yet children easily accomplish this task as they develop. Should less be demanded of adults?

Through Children's Minds

Foreword: Who Should Read This Book

Children are cherished in all societies but the same cannot be said of marketing and advertising professionals. And particularly not about those who market to children, an activity which many people consider unsavory and believe that the regulatory agencies should more vigorously confront.

Moreover, they insist, why should a company even bother to market to young people? They have minimal pocket money compared to adults, and behave inexplicably to their parents and less logically with strangers. If valid, these would be justified objections but they are not.

The truth is that children like most television commercials, which they consider thirty-second entertainment; and that they are far more sophisticated in their response to marketing than most people believe.

And while children do present a far smaller market than adults, their spending money is in the multi-billions of dollars and has increased tenfold over the past fifty years.

Children get money from their parents and relatives and the only people they have to spend it on is themselves. Adults have bills to pay but children only want to have fun. And while parents do buy most of a family's products, children and particularly teenagers direct many of these purchases. Also, few parents will buy food which they are sure that their children will not eat, and children often determine the restaurant where the family eats.

Through Children's Minds

Furthermore, children who become familiar with a brand may, as adults, be faithful customers for their products and to a child, who is a new customer, all brands are novel and so the youth market is continually fresh.

Shopping is an experience for children rather than an errand, an event and not a chore. And though often difficult to understand, there is a logic to children's behavior which readers of this book will learn along with guidelines in the marketing and creation of products which children value.

The belief that marketing to children is synonymous with exploitation is as false and simplistic as the notion that children believe all that they are told and are easily manipulated through advertising. Try telling *that* to the marketers of failed children's products! They have learned that children are smart and that you can't fool a child.

The purpose of marketing is to provide a product which satisfies a need. This is, for children, to see the product and think "Wow!" Even if parents, who control the purse strings, like a product and consider it wholesome, their positive feelings can be offset by the whining influence which children have on parents.

Through Children's Minds provides insight into the marketing and creation of children's products. After reading this book you will understand: what children value and why; the buying behavior of children, and how children influence adult purchases; why some children's products, television programs, and commercials are more successful than others; marketing in the global children's market; and the nature of market research

Through Children's Minds

with children.

But behaving ethically is equally important for a company's franchise is tenuous. If a children's product isn't advertised accurately or the parent feels that the company is just selling products and doesn't really care about their child, the child will be upset and their parents will be enraged, not only at that company but toward the entire industry.

So because every child is someone's child this book also includes ethical guidelines when marketing to children. These are crucial to consider to avoid causing harm, a public relations disaster, and possible government involvement.

This book is intended for manufacturers, product designers, and marketers of products for children between the age of three and twelve years though there is some information about teenagers too.

Readers who are seeking "recipes" to assure a successful product or marketing campaign will be disappointed for this is not possible. "By the numbers" creation does not usually work, as evidenced by the reported statement of the Disney executive after the disappointing opening sales of their 2013 movie, *The Lone Ranger*: "All the numbers looked good!"

But while promising that your product will become a hit is not possible, combining the insights which you gained from this book together with your creative imagination will make your success more likely.

Through Children's Minds

Introduction: How the Marketing To Children Began

We know much about how to market to adults. We know that adult shoppers prefer rounded to angular shaped packages for water, and that having pictures of what is inside are favored, these being on the right side of the package to ease left-to-right reading. We know that weight tends to be associated with quality (except perhaps with laptops), and that people associate cool colors with elegance.

But far less is known about youthful shoppers for while the marketing of products to adults is well accepted, the same is not true for children. They are believed helpless to resist smooth talk, even that which is ineptly delivered.

But this view, like many popular but false generalizations, is belied by the fact that to successfully market products to children, even those which their parents endorse, is enormously difficult. Many marketing managers will attest to this though, alas, following the loss of their job. This sorry event often occurs for just one reason: because the product or its marketing wasn't accurately tailored to the target's developmental level.

Market demand is rooted in broad social attitudes and practices. With the huge sums now being spent on marketing to children, it may be difficult to realize that the concept of childhood is a modern invention. In medieval time there was no separate status for children. They shared the same games with adults and lived their lives together. Children helped to support the family economy as soon as they could walk by working in the fields or being apprenticed. As late as the early nineteenth century, children as young as five worked

Through Children's Minds

alongside their parents in factories and mines.

The industrial revolution's values of hard work and seriousness undermined the legitimacy of games and sport as community rituals. Play became associated with innocence and childhood, and psychological immaturity was associated with children.

By the end of the nineteenth century, play was being described as the "stuff of childhood," how the young prepared for the world of work. Play was believed to socialize the young and harmlessly release their excess energy. It would rehearse them with the skills necessary for adulthood through enjoyable practice, and overcome their adjustment problems by working them out in fantasy.

Play became the socializing agent of the industrial era and toys were its tools. Teachers believed that play would foster concentration and obedience.

Play was to be the major teaching technique of early education. It would also be safer for children since learning with real objects could be hazardous, presenting dangers which could be avoided by using smaller, manageable toy cars and building material in *pretend play*. It was believed that children would be less resistant to being taught during play.

Parents often disparage toys and object to their influence. They are disturbed that a video game or branded doll can gain their child's attention far more readily than their parent's demand that they tidy their room, or play outdoors. To try to remedy this, parents involve their children in sports leagues or the Boy or Girl Scouts or other group activities. Yet it is difficult to exaggerate the effect of toys in a child's development since from their earliest months they serve as instruments with which to explore their environment and expand their abilities. They are also the first things that

Through Children's Minds

children learn they can control and can gain pleasure from.

Parents are a child's major socializing influence and what they purchase for their child is intended to influence them: books to encourage their love of reading and ideas; laptops and tablets and Smart Phones to acquaint them with current technology; designer clothes to "fit in" with their peers. These are intended to teach children the roles and ideas sanctioned by society.

But toys also serve a socializing role for the tool sets and dolls provide children with the rudiments of skills which will shape their lives. Though parents purchase these toys to express their love, it is largely the child who controls their use. This creative freedom through the use of their imagination, their *play instinct*, is what provides a toy's attractiveness. Indeed, should a toy which does not allow an imaginative element be considered a toy?

Both parents and teachers recognize the socializing influence of toys, permitting some and banning others such as toy guns. The influence of toys is powerful for much of children's thinking and interaction with their peers reflect their love of stories, possessions, and fantasy.

As the separate status of children became institutionalized, so did its commercialization by nineteenth century industry. Ads aroused anxiety in mothers by emphasizing the importance of manufactured foods as Shredded Wheat and proper (patent) medicines to a child's healthy development, with the child's need for maternal protection being stressed.

With increased industrialization and rising family incomes, manufactured children's goods became widely available. But these were mostly clothing and furniture with the parent and not the child being the marketing target.

During the 1920s and 1930s the concept of nuclear family entered the culture as a refuge from the harshness of industrial society. Men could find comfort at home: a setting which they ruled and was kept virtuous by their wife. This notion of family solidarity and the imagery of childhood was increasingly advertised to reduce the anxiety caused by the Great Depression. Ads provided a mirror into the more promising future which children would inhabit as illustrated by the modern technology of the radio and the airplane.

After World War II, children and domestic scenes became common in advertising. The special culture of children was emphasized along with their need for games and toys and learning equipment. A "good" parent provided these products with the implication that those parents who did not were failing.

Paradoxically, despite the widely advertised notion of a nuclear family, children's toys isolate the child by aiding their creation of a fantasy world of pleasure, a realm apart from family and societal constraints.

This separation was noted by the early, widely popular TV series, *Ozzie and Harriet,* in which the divergent viewpoints of parents and children were portrayed.

Psychologists began advising parents that it was normal for children to go through developmental stages during which they became increasingly competent, and the importance of allowing them the freedom to explore lest they eventually fail to gain the maturity expected of productive adults.

Joining this child-rearing turmoil, television contributed entertaining sitcoms which explored the intimacies of family life. Products could reduce family discontent and misunderstanding. There were foods and games which the entire family could enjoy, deodorants to prevent embarrassment, pet food to keep their dog healthy and content. The family could be unified through brand loyalty, gained through television's focus on consumerism.

These words are not intended to condemn television for parents have both positive and negative views of it. They recognize television's educational and babysitting value but condemn its effect in eroding family interaction because, being so hypnotic, it crowds out other experiences.

Yet today *family togetherness* has a different meaning. *Being together* means that family members are in earshot of one another and not, as in past decades, sitting close-by in one room. Parents feel better when their child is in their home and not in someone else's house even if each family member is doing their own thing.

The notion of family which television sitcoms fostered led to a segmentation of its marketing audience. Previously there had been little children's programming apart from Saturday morning cartoons. But later children's series, as on Nickelodeon, addressed children's concerns and interests and marketers began speaking directly to children.

Peer culture was wrapped into narratives in which conflicts were addressed and motives were explored, even if simplistically. From these shows, children gained information about social interaction and the world outside their neighborhood though there has been criticism that registration in the consumer world has been the primary focus of children's television.

Through Children's Minds

Chapter 1
What Children Are *Really* Like

All of us were once infants, and extraordinary creatures too. By the age of one, our neurological foundations for rational thinking, problem solving, and general reasoning were established. Earlier, by the age of six months, we learned the sounds of our native language and were soon to begin grasping its grammatical structure.

To foster this development, children require not only love but talkative, coherent parents (or caregivers) who, through language and eye contact, relate to children as individuals. This interaction fosters the growth of the wiring patterns in the brain which make us fully human, creating neurons which grow and travel into distant areas of the brain and await further instructions.

This progress follows no master plan. Instead, these parts self-organize, being acutely sensitive to environmental conditions as the pieces are put into place.

Who we are depends on where we once were for these experiences lay down the physical basis of what we call *intelligence*. The ability to function in our advanced society does not simply happen, and *play* is an important part in this development.

Sociability is one of our basic characteristics. This fact caused Aristotle to describe the human being as "a social animal." Social skills appear in earliest infancy: babies can recognize familiar people at three months of age.

Pretend play enables children to take on different roles, to experience the emotions of others and be better able to tell what another person is feeling. Playing "doctor" or "tea party" helps them to learn the rituals of behavior in social settings. This includes the notion of turn-taking: that after taking their turn they should pause to allow their playmate to react.

Children learn that behavior has context, that its meaning depends on the context, and that behavior can be commented on. Criticism and evaluation make art and science possible so play has an important innovative function. By imagining how things might be, children gain flexibility too.

Play teaches not only cooperation but also competition: about rules and team spirit and the different feelings association with winning and losing.

The eminent psychoanalyst, Erik Erikson, considered play to be the childhood form of the human ability to deal with experience. The child does this by creating model situations of reality and mastering them through experimentation and planning. Through their mastery over objects, children permit themselves to imagine that they are masters of their life difficulties too.

The noted clinical psychologist, Bruno Bettelheim, recommended that children be encouraged to play out their inner feelings and thoughts in order to gain mastery over them and to give harmless expression to unconscious ideas. He felt that non-dangerous play should not be censored and, to some degree, that parents should let children play by themselves and with their peers.

The world renowned developmental psychologist, Jean Piaget, stressed that, while playing, children are building basic intellectual structures which serve their cognitive growth and are indispensable to their healthy development.

Albert Einstein considered Piaget's principle, that

Through Children's Minds

children think differently from adults, as being "so simple that only a genius could have thought of it." And Piaget discovered much more.

According to Piaget, the brain is not a passive receptacle but an active, organizing system. Every input, every experience, is run through the brain's existing cognitive structures, both changing and being changed by those structures. All thinking is *action* though not in a physical sense. The brain conducts *operations*, an operation being an action that has become abstract. *Because the brain is naturally active, the motivation to learn is internal and external reward is not required.*

When a child experiences a new situation they consider it in terms of the mental actions, or cognitive structures, that they bring to that situation. These cognitive structures, or understandings or principles, organize the new knowledge but may also be changed by it and this is the essence of mental development.

If the input precisely fits the established cognitive structures then learning (change) *will not occur*. Nor will change occur if the input is so different that it does not fit within the cognitive structures at all. Change only occurs when the complexity of the child's cognitive structure *doesn't quite match* the input.

In other words, *a learning task must be a little bit harder, but not too difficult, for the child's learning and involvement to occur.* This principle explains how to be an effective teacher though Piaget studied cognitive structures and not practical applications.

Very early in life these actions occur through the physical exploration of objects, by *playing* with them. Later these play objects become *internalized*, symbolized by representations of these objects. Finally, these symbols, and the principles underlying how they should be related to, become organized into the complex mental

Through Children's Minds

network that underlies and enables logical adult thinking. This fully developed structure has also learned how to learn most efficiently.

Despite the enormous developmental tasks which confront newborns, parents need not worry that they are making mistakes for the human brain is a miraculous structure awaiting only that care and interaction which nearly all parents provide. There is a wide range of experiences which support healthy emotional and mental development. Difficulties develop only when what is required is gravely lacking, far outside the range of experiences needed to foster the development of biologically healthy children.

So parents shouldn't worry if they haven't taught their baby numerical concepts or an extensive vocabulary. All that a child requires is an ongoing dialogue with adult speech for words are a lure and the catalyst in the development of a child's thinking and reasoning skills. This constant child-parent patter is the single most important factor in early brain development. The reason why the children of professional parents score highest on intelligence tests is because these parents provide their children with the most spoken language.

Tone and affirmative feedback are important too. The mind of a child who hears, "What did we do today?" will develop far differently than the child who always hears, "Stop that!" The latter children will learn to use language and to say complex sentences but not to deal with language in the most conceptual manner.

Psychologists have known that these deficiencies are avoidable for decades. As has long been said, providing only love is not enough.

Fifty years ago a British researcher at University College, London, Basil Bernstein, related the difficulty in teaching working class children as contrasted with those from middle-class backgrounds, despite their comparable intelligence level on non-verbal intelligence tests, to the distinction between what he called "public language" and "formal language" though their use did not predominate for every child.

The characteristics of public language include the use of short, grammatically simple, often unfinished sentences with the frequent use of personal pronouns and a limited use of adjectives. Many statements signal a requirement for the previous speech sequence to be reinforced, as by asking "Wouldn't it?" and "You see?"

With public language, curiosity is limited and focused by the relatively low level of conceptualization. The concern with the immediate tends to make difficult the development of a reflective experience.

In contrast, formal language contains accurate grammatical order and sentences which include a wide range of adjectives and adverbs without the use of dominant words or phrases.

The use of formal language gives direction to the organization of thinking and feelings whereas a public language is more concerned with membership within a group toward which there is a strong sense of loyalty, it containing a "we versus them" attitude when relating to outsiders.

The predominant use of public language cripples the ability of children to function in an adult, technological society for when teachers demand that these children use language differently, that they precisely describe their individual experiences using an expansive vocabulary, the children experience these requests differently than when they are made of a formal language user.

For the formal language user it is a situation of *linguistic development* while for the public language user it is one of *linguistic change* and arouses feelings of bewilderment, isolation, and defenselessness. This educational demand, which is essential, has the effect of alienating the child from their origins.

A teacher's task is not simple, or easy.

For many years we didn't know much about children apart from what is obvious. That they cannot be relied on to report their behavior dependably, and have poor recall. In some areas there is little systematic information at all. We know little about the sexual knowledge of children because most parents and schools will not allow researchers to find out. And even those crucial questions which mental health clinicians are required to ask of all new patients including children, whether they experience suicidal or homicidal thoughts, is viewed suspiciously. Parents fear that asking these questions will insert unwelcome ideas into their child's mind though the fact is that a child who possesses such troubling thoughts welcomes discussing them and the relief that follows.

Yet there are other reasons why so much less is known about marketing to children than marketing to adults: for a long time there was little business interest in doing so. Many managers didn't consider children to constitute a large enough market to conduct expensive, thorough research though children spend more than thirty-two billion dollars a year and influence their parents' purchase of more than one-hundred-and-fifty-five billion dollars a year. There was also a perception factor: as with parents, many executives believed it inappropriate to consider children as a market.

But times have changed and now children are studied both as a consumer and how they interact with the family consumer unit. Still, even today, many adults consider the major differences between children and

Through Children's Minds

adults to be those which psychologists consider superficial: that children are smaller than adults, and know less; and that they are more spontaneous and more likely to be excited by events which adults ignore.

Recently, while waiting on line in a crafts store, two hugely smiling girls of about three stood before me. Both were entranced by the small toy with which one of them played and excitedly demonstrated.

It was the fundamental differences in thinking between adults and children, and not superficialities, which Jean Piaget studied.

How do children think differently from adults? Does this mean that if a book is placed before a three-year-old he might call it a car? Or is this difference evidenced by a five-year-old boy who, upon being asked by his mother why he hit his sister moments before, responded angrily, "I *didn't* hit her!"

Because the minds of children develop at a far greater rate than ever again in life, certain psychological characteristics exist in abundance: curiosity and being open to new experiences; the search for challenges, and to master them; the attempt to develop a greater sense of who they are or, as psychologists term it, gain a greater *sense of self*; and, most importantly, gaining new capacities and learning the limits of these.

A product which is considered by children to fulfill one or all of these needs will be desired by them. And because this product fosters the child's psychological development, marketing it calls for no apology.

Some present advertising harkens back to the mythical America of generations ago with its stably working father, stay-at-home mother, and their contented, unworried children. The pictures and calendars of Norman Rockwell which portray such scenes still sell though the magazines which publicized them, as

Through Children's Minds

The Saturday Evening Post, have long since disappeared.

While some of the differences between then and today are widely known, as that far fewer family units today contain two parents, another change is surprising: the degree to which children influence family purchase decisions.

A survey found that the purchase of toys is influenced by sixty-one percent of children, and that of breakfast cereal by sixty-eight percent of children, while the family purchase of candy and snacks is influenced by fifty-five percent of children. No wonder that ads for these products account for three-quarter of all television ads on Saturday morning, which is the most popular viewing time for very young children.

But children also influence the purchase of adult goods: almost twenty-five percent of nine-year-olds to fifteen-year-olds who were surveyed said that they influenced the type of TV which their parents purchased, nineteen percent influenced the brand of car, fourteen percent influenced the kind of computer, and thirty-eight percent influenced the purchase of bread, with more than half stating that they disagreed with their parent's brand choice of grocery items.

With figures like these, it is not surprising that, in one study, eighty-two percent of children between the age of six and fifteen said that their major wish was to have more money to buy things; and nearly one-third of them said that they thought making a lot of money would be important when they became adults. This goal came ahead of marriage or having children.

Thus, companies became more interested in studying youth as a market for several reasons: for themselves, since children purchase many billions of dollars of goods a year; as an important factor of

Through Children's Minds

influence, since they effect the purchases of their friends and family; and because youth represent a future market, developing tastes and purchasing habits at an early age ("If we can get children to believe that X is a good product then they will buy it as adults.")

In a sense, children can be considered to be an ideal marketer's target for several reasons. Children spend almost everything they earn (or are given) and don't comparison shop; they don't necessarily make logical purchasing decisions; they are passionate television and Internet viewers; and they are subject to intense peer pressure. Moreover, many children today are the offspring of guilt-ridden, working parents with more income to lavish on increasingly fewer children.

But with these advantages comes the major drawback that a disappointed child can become a beacon of disappointment: a customer who will widely express their feelings in this Internet age, causing a company to lose far more than one customer since children tend naturally to repeat things.

As children grow older, they become increasingly savvy about advertising and ever more resentful of being talked down to or lied to. They want facts, not because they care about things like nutrition or durability but because they know that their parents do and that they will need this information to sell them on a product.

Marketers who consider children to be stupid or naïve are making a big mistake.

Through Children's Minds

Through Children's Minds

Chapter 2

The Behavior of the Child As Customer

While many people enjoy shopping, this attitude is not universal. Researchers have found that about twenty percent of adults have hostile feelings to anything related to shopping. These attitudes, like many important ones, develop in childhood. More sensitive marketing can reduce the likelihood of these negative attitudes forming.

I recently noted an incident with an infant. The father had handed his daughter a toy, which the child pushed away. She wanted it placed farther back so she would have to reach for it.

Why did this child, and other children, behave like this? Because they possess the innate need to expand their capacities and test their abilities with new experiences.

Children learn to shop by accompanying their parents into the colorful marketplace of commotion and choice. Seated in a shopping cart, separate from but still close enough to their parent for comfort, the child explores a new world of opportunity: food and other products which they enjoy and through which their parents express their love. Even toddlers make primitive associations between products and stores and advertisements. But children *are* difficult to shop with and some supermarkets have gained customer loyalty by providing low-cost child-care centers.

Slowly, though perhaps too rapidly for some, the child begins making demands, these deriving from their experiences and from advertisements which they have seen or heard of from friends.

From the interaction between information and product and parental guidance ("This product is better."

Through Children's Minds

"I don't like that brand."), children increase their ability to make choices, a skill which is essential to their functioning as adults and not only for goods.

Stores and products become favored by children because of their comfort level and parental attitudes. The brain changes most rapidly in early childhood and stores provide an abundance of experiences to feed this development. Under their parent's watchful eyes, the child leaves the safety of the shopping cart to find intriguing products which they can reach for and touch. Meanwhile, their parent educates them about health and nutrition and cost. Concepts which are elementary to adults, as that ten dollars is more costly than five dollars and what this means, must first be learned.

By permitting children to purchase products, though under supervision, the child gains a sense of independence and power. This experience lends an indelible impression and, depending on the attitude of store personnel, can create positive or negative memories which persist.

There is a large gas station/convenience store near my office where children often buy treats and later excitedly describe their purchases to me.

The importance of the marketer in the success of a product cannot be over-emphasized. It is they who must decide upon the proper advertisement and display which, because children are dependent, must meet with a favorable response from parents too.

This is not a simple task. Just as some parents would benefit from learning to perform their parenting role better, so would some marketers who market to children. Few would respond accurately to all of the following questions.

A mall based retail store manager who wanted to increase sales to children put up brightly colored signs

Through Children's Minds

reading, "WE LOVE CHILDREN." Would this store realize: (1) No increase in sales to children; (2) A reduction in overall sales; (3) Puzzlement among their sales staff, (4) All of the above. The correct response is (4).

A manager who presses for the marketing of a children's product based on their personal childhood memories will likely soon: (1) Be unemployed; (2) Be promoted; (3) Change careers; (4) Any of the above. The most correct answer is (1) but, because of the quirks of office politics, (4) may also be correct.

Marketers who ignore parental attitudes when marketing to children are: (1) Skilled marketers; (2) Knowledgeable about children; (3) Behaving in a highly risky manner; (4) Doomed to fail. The correct answers are (3) and (4).

The Brand Manager System, when imposed on children's products, is: (1) *What system?* (2) Excellent, as it is with adult products; (3) Sometimes productive; (4). Inappropriate. The correct answer is (4).

Children enjoy shopping because: (1) Shopping enables children to practice more mature behavior; (2) Shopping enables children to satisfy their needs; (3) Shopping enables children to function more independently; (4) All of the above. The correct answer is (4).

Children's toys: (1) Mimic adult culture; (2) Celebrate rebellion against parental restrictions; (3) Encourage the development of a child's unique identity; (4) All of the above. The correct answer is (4).

Clearly, successfully marketing products to children requires more than just instinct (though this element should not be ignored!) and is a complex endeavor.

Through Children's Minds

Chapter 3

The Psychology of the Child As Customer

While the career of the celebrated developmental psychologist, Jean Piaget, had nothing to do with marketing, understanding his great insights about children is essential to marketing their products. But to follow his basic principle, that the thinking of children is fundamentally different from that of adults, the marketer must understand the world of children. They must, with one part of their mind, think like a child while the adult portion of their mind freely associates to this experience.

Precisely what did Piaget mean when he insisted that children think differently than adults? Piaget argued that intelligence develops in a series of stages. These are related to age and are progressive because one stage must be accomplished before the next stage can occur.

At each stage of development the child forms a view of reality which is appropriate for their age. Piaget conceived of intellectual development as being an upwardly expanding spiral in which children must constantly reconstruct the ideas formed at earlier levels with new, higher order concepts acquired at the next level of development.

Piaget defined four stages of cognitive development. The first, Sensorimotor Stage, lasts from birth to two years. During this stage, infants learn from the movements they make and the sensations that result from them. They gain the realization that they exist apart from objects, that they can cause things to happen, and they acquire *object constancy*, the realization that objects exist even when they cannot see them.

The second, Preoperational Stage, lasts from two through seven years and begins when the child gains language. Their thinking is egocentric, they feeling that everyone sees things as they do, and they begin to use symbols to represent objects. They can count and sort objects according to their similarity, and distinguish past from present from future, though their focus remains primarily on the present. They have not yet gained the capacity for abstract thinking.

The third, Concrete Operational Stage, lasts from seven through eleven years. During this stage, children can see things from the point of view of others, and imagine events outside of their lives. They become capable of some logical thought processes, as that an object can belong to several categories simultaneously, can be both blue and large, or that a person can be bad in certain ways but also good in others. Thus, children begin to view matters in other than black or white terms.

The fourth and final stage, the Formal Operational Stage, begins at adolescence and extends throughout adulthood. Now children can reason in more abstract ways, can test hypotheses using logic and focus on possibilities.

While there has been criticism of Piaget's theories, particularly that the stages which he describes are so discrete, there is no question that the thought processes of children and adults are fundamentally difficult.

There are other basic cognitive capacities which humans develop. These include the ability to distinguish reality from fantasy or, as psychologists say, to do "reality testing"; the ability to modulate mood so that it does not quickly fluctuate from feeling "high" to feeling "low"; and the ability to so control thinking that one's speech and behavior make sense.

While these capacities are not inborn, the human mind is genetically programmed to develop them. This occurs naturally provided that the child experiences a

Through Children's Minds

"good enough" parenting which does not, however, mean *perfect* parenting. If this is absent, deficiencies in one or more of these abilities may occur with the child experiencing problems in learning, in interacting with their peers, and in later adult functioning.

In real life these developments do not happen in stark terms. The weakness of these basic cognitive abilities may range from minimal, in which case the child's later life is largely unaffected, to so great that the child may never grow to function independently. Still, regardless of these factors, all children relate to the shopping experience in childlike and not adult ways.

Children enter the shopping world young and with eyes that light up, most children having been taken shopping by the age of six months. They first observe the colorful objects, then handle them, then request that they be purchased, and finally become independent shoppers. All children go through this process though, in single parent families, children become independent consumers earlier than do children in two-parent households. It is because this learning process is independent of social class, family income, or education, that children can be treated as a mass market.

Let us try to imagine ourselves as a child: first as a five-year-old boy, Billy, and then as a teenage girl, Maryanne. Billy has now entered kindergarten and this, for him, is an entirely different world even if he had earlier attended several hours of pre-school daily.

He must now awake on a rigid schedule for five days a week and then ride a school bus accompanied by other children, many of whom are likely strangers. Just like the bus driver who is far less tolerant toward misbehavior than are his parents.

At school, there are other rules that Billy must follow with implicit threats if he disobeys: being isolated from his classmates, or receiving a scolding from the principal who can make critical comments to his mother and which will create more stress for him.

Intermittently, throughout the day, there are limited breaks from these rigidities: during lunchtime, playground recess, and the nap which he may not need but is forced to take.

Despite these pressures, Billy enjoys school for the social and educational interactions provide him with more of the experiences which his mind requires for it to mature. This enjoyment is created by *effectance motivation*: the good feeling that the mind *naturally experiences* when it is expanding and effectively using its capacities.

But Billy needs relaxation too and one way which he gains this is by shopping. Not for the essentials of food and clothing which everyone needs to live but for those which further feed his mind through its imaginative capacity. After school and gaining the snack which he demands (for his parents are far more agreeable to his requests than is his teacher), Billy accompanies his parent on one of their shopping trips.

Though feeling fearful at being towered over by adults, he conceals this through a blustering façade and, if necessary, a tantrum. While some specialty stores, those which sell shoes and clothing, bore him, supermarkets and especially toy stores do not. Here, there are further experiences which engage his mind and imagination.

Now being five, Billy no longer rides in the shopping cart but accompanies his parent as they walk the aisles. He notices the different shapes and bright colors of the wares. The shelves of cereal and snack products beckon for their packages contain figures which he knows from the Nickelodeon programs he watches:

Through Children's Minds

how SpongeBob and Patrick got lost and found adventure on a family trip, and of Patrick taking a break from the hubbub of his daily life with pampering from SpongeBob, while Karen and Plankton and Mr. Krabs and Sandy deal with other troubles.

While Billy is intermittently involved with the difficulties of these fictional characters, he imagines himself loading up a shopping cart with goods which he chooses, a thought made easier by the scaled-down carts which many stores provide, knowing that children have money to spend and parents who are ever willing to indulge them.

But because Billy is a child with immature capacities, his confidence is more feigned than real. At any moment, when confronted by a new situation, the pain of anxiety can intrude, perhaps from a demanding store clerk or a stranger who rudely objects to his antics. The pain exists until his parent soothes the situation.

Adults buy goods which meet their needs but children buy goods to satisfy their soul. While this statement is too general to be completely accurate, there is truth to it because of their different life roles. An adult must purchase what they need to live but a child's basic needs for food and clothing and other necessities are provided by their parents. Thus, thoughts of other goods fill their mind: those whose shape or color or packaging attract their attention, or products which enable identification with friends or the gaining of an identity separate from adults.

And because children think differently from adults, their manner of relating to shopping also differs.

For children, unlike with adults, the issue of price is negligible. If a child wants something, they want it regardless of its price or the financial ability of their parents to buy it. The relationship between price and

Through Children's Minds

desirability and family income and purchase capacity is one which must be learned.

The time frame of children is also different. An adult may willingly and understandingly save for months to purchase a desired item, unlike young children for whom even minutes can be too painful to wait.

The logic which applies to purchases by adults is absent from children. An adult who has decided to buy a four door, hybrid, "family" auto for definite reasons (need for a car which can comfortably seat four and gets good gas mileage) will not change their mind and choose a two-seater sport car because of a commercial which they loved. This is unlike a child whose mind can change quickly, not from lack of intelligence but because the child's mind is continually in flux and developing rapidly whereas the adult's mind is mature and fully developed.

This great difference between the child's and adult's mind creates a major difference between how one must market to each group: marketing towards the adult can be relatively unchanging while with the child one is dealing with a moving market.

When concerned with teenagers one must remember that, though possessing a largely adult body, the adolescent mind contains both child *and* adult elements. The concept of adolescence is relatively modern: only in 1904 did adolescence become a recognized, discrete stage of life instead of being considered simply a brief transition between child and adult. Even the term "teenager" didn't come into use until 1939.

The ability to relate to others and to consider their viewpoints when making decisions develops slowly from childhood onward and is incomplete throughout the teenage years. Added to this is the relatively limited knowledge which teenagers have of the world. I have met

Through Children's Minds

a literal handful of teenagers who follow the news and teenagers' knowledge of recent historic events, even of major wars and political figures, tends to be minimal. This has been described as "cultural ignorance."

While the child and adolescent orientations differ, there are similarities. With both levels of development, self-interest is primary and their purchases are partly intended to set themselves apart from others: that they be viewed as having a particular identity as a member of their own special group, whether child or teenager. Adults have no need for this since, as both children and teenagers accurately believe, adults control the world.

The fictional characters which youth enjoy and choose also reflect their age. The younger the child, the less likely the figure is chosen to reflect adult interests such as career and married life and parenthood.

Parents need not fear the common interest of children in toy guns or of teenagers in video games which portray the world exploding. Because both groups would be unable to survive without the assistance of adults, it is only natural that they experience fear. But, not recognizing that the source of this fear is internal and reflects real personal inadequacies, their mind behaves as it normally does to rid itself of pain: it *projects* the source of the fear outward. Thus the reason for their anxiety is perceived by them not as reflecting their actual inadequacy but real danger in the world. Which a toy gun, or video play, can symbolically reduce through fantasy and provide comfort.

I feel the need to add this cautious, obvious note: that toy guns which only make noise are far safer than those which propel objects.

Similarly, the common teenage dream of blowing up the world reflects not their unconscious homicidal tendency but their desire to reject the constraints of adult

Through Children's Minds

society and to create a wholly new world. But, though laudable, this attempt is doomed to fail because of the adolescent's inadequate knowledge and experience.

Earlier in human history, the creation and telling of stories was how acceptable behavior and cultural values were transmitted across generations. First, through the oral word and then the written word with digital and audio books being merely the latest means.

Age old fairy tales inform children that though difficulties are unavoidable, success is assured by being resolute. A point of view which, though impressive, is what many adults would declare to be a true fairy tale since luck and advantage play significant roles in life. Still, fairy tales and commercial stories provide structure within which a child can place their experiences and align their life.

Prior to the nineteenth century, children's books were written to teach religious values and instill moral instruction. Only later were books created to serve as a source of pleasure, this leading to greater literacy. Like toys, books also serve to separate the individual from their community and foster independent thinking.

Before the widespread availability of books, literacy was less prized and both children and adults were illiterate. But as literacy become a requirement for entrance into the adult world, learning to read became a necessity for children.

Through increasing sales, publishers realized that children experience the world differently than adults. They responded to this with fiction that challenged parental authority and gave enjoyment to the challenge of gaining literacy. The comic books of recent times, with their links between text and pictures, have historical roots in the illustrated medieval editions of *Aesop's Fables*.

Through Children's Minds

The comic strip of the late nineteenth century was the only part of newspapers which could be enjoyed by both adults and children, and they evolved into the modern comic books. Many of the most popular comic strips, such as *Little Orphan Annie,* represented the growing concern with raising children.

The publishing industry's interest in creating comic books began with their recognition that children don't have enough money to buy books on their own but could afford ten cents a comic. These visual narratives told the adventures of the Superman and Dick Tracy and Buck Rogers characters, invincible heroes who could surmount extraordinary dangers, situations which appeal to children's heroic imagination.

That comics weren't completely accepted is evidenced by the 1950s congressional hearings and the book by Frederic Wertham, *Seduction of the Innocents.* Both portrayed comic books as providing education in crime and ghoulish behavior.

Yet the adding of adventure, excitement, and family and peer conflict to children's books began in the nineteenth century. *Alice in Wonderland* sold forty-five thousand copies within its first ten years and sells robustly today aided, paradoxically, by the introduction of comic books. Their sale revealed that children, by purchasing books on their own, could constitute a separate market and that even if comic books were valueless, a higher class of fiction which appealed to children was possible. While promoting literacy, these books also helped introduce consumerism into the children's culture.

The change in genre from fairy tale to early novel to comic strip and comic book to television sitcom, video game, and to the Japanese manga and anime merely reflect the change in children's culture.

Through Children's Minds

Yet by expanding the channels of marketing into the imagination of children, publishers bred seeds which, ultimately, reduced their market as television and movies and video games began competing for the child's attention and gained the interest of other marketers.

Chapter 4
Why Children Buy

While many adult purchases are of necessities, children buy things because they enjoy shopping for nowhere else can they make so many decisions. In school or at home, children are told what to do and even if given a choice these are limited: would they prefer a turkey sandwich or pizza for lunch in the school cafeteria?

But in a store, one that caters to young people, the adult clerks seek to satisfy their smallest whim and children learn to express these early.

One four-year-old girl was taken by her mother for a haircut. "I want it streaked," she said. "Oh, I don't know how to do that," the attendant replied. "Well then, get me someone who can!" the child demanded.

For children, the store provides an assortment of colors and tastes and experiences within their grasp. Whatever they want can be theirs, if they can convince their parents to buy it.

Parents are often surprised by the powerful emotions which children's possessions attain. One ten-year-old boy threatened to run away if his video game player was taken away. Would a rational adult act similarly if their cable TV were shut off?

Children possess such feelings because of their limited awareness. They live in the present with little consideration of their future. If asked, they can usually state the type of work they would like to do when they become adult but this is in the realm of fantasy. For children, the present and not future events is what is real.

A possession like a video game player can arouse such intense emotion within a child for it provides them not only enjoyment and relaxation but a venue within which they can relieve feelings and try on adult roles, experiences which are needed for their healthy psychological development.

Children want to become adult for they sense their limitations. This is why they resent being termed "children." As one child said, "Why do you call this a baby aspirin? I'm not a baby!"

Children are not born consumers. They learn this role, mostly through experiences with their parents but also through their experiences with marketers. As children become more independent, the influence of marketers grows. But while the influence of parents wanes, this is the greatest influence over a child, even with teenagers for whom the peer group becomes important. Only for adolescents with emotional difficulties may their peer group gain unbeatable influence. Thus for marketers to ignore parents and attend solely to their child customers is a risky endeavor.

Parents try to help their children make wise decisions but this educational effort is scattered amongst other parental activities. Parents are busy and children learn independently from many sources. A parent may prefer a particular store but if the child views this store as being unfriendly, the parent's attitude will not be adopted, and the preferred shopping venue will likely change for the parent too.

Parents believe that it is their responsibility to educate their child and are loathe to recognize the influence of others, feeling that this brands them as an inadequate parent. For this reason they may become angry when their child spontaneously sings an advertising jingle or repeats a catchy advertising phrase, fearing this foreign influence on *their* family.

But, as will be continually stressed in this book, children are not dumb or easily influenced, and the

Through Children's Minds

influence of their parents remains powerful throughout their life. An eighty-five year old woman, a renowned academician, bemoaned that her deceased mother had not learned of her latest, highest public award.

While some consumer education is provided by teachers, it is not systematic or consistent across school systems. The teachers may be poorly prepared and the subject considered a frill in these days of tightening school budgets.

Children become educated as consumers but slowly, which is how they gain other skills. Psychologists now know that infants and toddlers have far greater capacities than had been believed and that these early insights become engrained within their personality structure. The persistence of these early conclusions is why the human personality is so difficult to change. The ancient adage, "give me the child until they are seven and I will give you the man," recognized this truth.

So from the time that the infant is placed in a shopping cart and accompanies their parent, impressions are gained about shopping. That shopping involves choosing and making decisions with some products being lingered over while others are quickly picked. That shopping can be a comfortable or difficult experience. That people in the store are workers or shoppers and that these strangers may be friendly or unfriendly and are generally ignored.

All of these facts are fuel for the child's developing mind, along with associations between satisfying products and stores, these beginning to include advertisements about the age of two.

As the number of store visits increase and children learn through advertising of a greater number of products to desire, they begin making purchasing demands of their parents. They learn ways to increase their likelihood of success, initially through tantrums and tears and later by using sophisticated wheedling methods to foster parental feelings of guilt.

Not recognizing these as being a normal developmental phase, embarrassing public tantrums may foster anti-marketing sentiment among parents, an attitude which children then adopt.

By asking for and gaining products within a store, the child begins to adopt the role of consumer and gains capacities which become increasingly crucial in negotiating the adult world. What college should I go to? Am I being told the truth about the value of this career? Even, is this the individual who I should marry?

All relationships involve negotiating what must be given for what will be gained

It is natural for the mind to create shortcuts to most quickly negotiate its environment and the toddler learns these too: that a store is where you buy things; that a freezer is cold and holds a special type of food while shelves contain other products which lay along different aisles; and that while such good foods as milk and ice cream can be found in a convenience store, parents do not buy much food there because these stores are generally more expensive.

These conclusions are so ingrained in adults that many consider children to have been born with them. Yet each of these facts must be learned, and children in other cultures must learn similar facts too.

About the age of three to four years, children begin to walk by their parent's side and to ask to buy products. This is a normal phase in the greater developmental task of the child becoming increasingly independent of their parents. Children may adopt particular brands though this preference, like many at that young age, may not endure, and be as much a function of the striking package as what it contains.

The shopping experience is used by many parents to educate their children on the process of shopping and the need to make wise decisions, with the important issues of cost and nutrition and safety being covered. Through these experiences the child learns to become a consumer who is increasingly able to care for themselves, which is a crucial task on their path toward adulthood.

During these shopping experiences, the child's psychological connections between advertisement and product and fulfillment of desire and store develop, becoming engrained and strengthened by the pleasure which children gain from contact with their parents.

There is one more insight which children must gain: to understand the role of money in the shopping process, and that one object can be exchanged for another with something desirable being gained rather than lost. Though adults also consider this insight to be basic, it nevertheless is one which must be learned for the young child does not yet understand the concepts of exchange and money.

But children learn this quickly for they sense that buying is an adult activity and they very much want to leave childhood and become adults.

Children continually seek to acquire needed skills, and the learning of reading and arithmetic is not enough to assure success in the social system. The child needs other skills, many of which are gained through attendance at such feasting events as birthday parties and holiday celebrations and during visits to friends' homes.

Thus children's interest in the consumer culture is far more than simple hedonism or greed or passivity: it involves the desires for community, freedom from adult authority, seriousness, and goal directedness. And, as a mass culture, toys and television give children a medium of communication.

The complexity of the shopping experience arouses stress during the gaining of the needed abilities. It is not a simple matter for the child to give the (provided by their parent) money to the sales clerk in exchange for the product which the child desires for this task involves risk. Will the clerk be friendly or humiliate them, and what should they do then? What if they become so frightened that they start crying or, from even greater fright, wet themselves? What should they do if the clerk ignores them?

Adults quickly forget how inadequate they were during childhood.

A crucial task of early childhood is for the child to develop an identity independent of their parents. And while there is truth to the old saying that a chestnut doesn't fall far from the tree, that the influence of parents is profound, each child is unique and seeks their individual identity. Shopping for goods is one of the ways that they do this.

The preference for certain TV shows and toys sets children apart from their elders. Children feel that their particular knowledge and interests grant them power for they know about things of which their parents are ignorant.

But because children cannot purchase objects or watch television without their parents' assistance or approval, they are necessarily involved and may disapprove of their children's desires. Thus when the child is very young, battle lines are already being drawn between parents and children over snacks and toys and media.

Chapter 5

How Child Customers Differ From Adult Customers

While you are reading these pages, and in every nation, some children are being abused. This may seem an odd statement to place in a book on marketing to children but it is relevant since the same reason underlies both parental abuse and why a children's product fails: because children are not understood as what they are.

The following example, how the misunderstanding of an adult led to horrendous consequences, will clarify how a child and an adult can view an identical situation completely differently.

A parent demanded that their child clean their room, which they failed to do. The parent repeated their demand with the same result. Now enraged, the adult struck out and hit their child who falls and strikes their head on the edge of the dresser. He then lays, bleeding and unconscious, on the floor.

You can imagine the rest: the Emergency Medical Services workers arrive, the child is transported to the hospital and the police are notified, the parent is arrested, and the state's Child Protective Services becomes involved.

Why did these sorry, unnecessary events happen? Because the parent did not realize that a child's mind is far different from an adult's, and that this can cause each to relate to the identical situation differently.

This is how far too many parents would view the situation: they are the parent and master or mistress of the household, their child is in a lesser position and must obey orders. A parent who cannot gain obedience from their child is a failure as a parent. The parent's feeling of

Through Children's Minds

frustration, and the anger which arose from it, might cause them to strike out in order to show the child who the boss in the family *really was* lest the parent lose complete authority.

But a child would view the same situation differently. To a child, cleaning their room is not a priority. They might have had a nightmare the night before which still troubled them, or there might have been a dispute with a friend which was yet to be resolved. The child realized their inadequacy and inability to function alone in the adult world. They knew who the boss in the house was and that it was not them. But a child rarely says this when they are upset. Instead, they behave in a puzzling way, and often by being defiant. This is why one of the most frequent mental health diagnoses for both children and teenagers is Oppositional Defiant Disorder, which is symptomatized by refusing to comply with adult requests, and being deliberately annoying.

Just as both this child and their parent viewed the "clean room" situation in a dissimilar manner, they consider other life experiences differently too.

Most pressing adult concerns have no relevance to a child. These, for the typical adult, are to be healthy and not ill, to be relaxed and not tense, to control their life and not be at the mercy of events. Yet while every child also wants to be healthy, relaxed, and to control their life, these are not their conscious concerns. Being greatly limited in abilities and dependent, they rely on their parents to deal with these unspoken needs and the marketer who emphasizes adult issues to children is doomed to fail.

Yet there *are* similarities between child and adult customers. With both, purchases are made, or their purchase is influenced, to satisfy what they believe will be a better life toward which they consciously or

Through Children's Minds

unconsciously strive. Only because this concept of "better life" is hazy can marketing be successful.

Children have motives and priorities which, though different from those of adults, are equally powerful: to have fun, and to fulfill their genetically ingrained desires to use and further develop their physical and mental abilities. This arouses *intrinsic motivation,* which is a different but powerful type of "fun."

Being inherently efficient, the mind automatically places situations and people into categories for this speeds up the time which it needs to make decisions. Thus we have pre-determined that walking down dark streets at 1:00AM is more dangerous than doing so at noon, and that a man carrying a machete while walking in a city is best avoided.

Adults do not simply buy objects. They follow *rules* when behaving as a consumer, many of which are not conscious, having been unconsciously gained early in childhood. This action is performed in a manner similar to how children become able to speak their native tongue grammatically: because, when toddlers, each person deduces the grammatical structure of their nation's language. The brain is indeed a remarkable creation!

Thus, early in their development, a child gains information with which they construct *consumer behavior rules* which are unique to them and organize their shopping experiences.

They learn the value of money and where products can be purchased. They learn that they need to categorize future purchases by their desirability. They learn that they can influence the purchases of their parents and with which category of goods they will be most influential. They learn the concept of a brand, its association with quality, and the degree to which it

Through Children's Minds

should influence a purchase. These *rules* are based on parental instruction and advertising.

Children also learn to "shop around" by discussing products with their parents and friends and by viewing store displays. They distinguish stores with personnel that are helpful and friendly to children from those which are not.

The other consumer elements of adult behavior are present in a child but in less advanced form: the child being aware of a product but not how it can fulfill their needs and so not seeking it; the child holding back their desire for a product because of the attitude of their parents toward it (such as a toy gun), or because the child is being punished; or, simply, the unavailability of a purchase because of the family's lack of money.

Some products are purchased for children not because of their desire but from the parent's nostalgia for something which is far from their child's radar. This old product evokes powerful feelings in their parent who assumes, only sometimes correctly, that their child will love it too.

A consumer motive shared by both children and adults is the purchase of a product to present an image or to identify with a group: branded sneakers for a child, or a hybrid car for their parents.

A person is not always conscious of what they need and advertising capitalizes on this. This is sometimes for a commendable purpose as with the recommendation to live a healthier lifestyle. Other times it is to create an entirely new industry. Deodorant products began, and had their greatest period of sale, in the 1930s when the idea that bodily odor was unhealthy and its association with uncultured behavior was spread. The sale of handkerchiefs began its steady decline following the advertising slogan, "Don't put a cold in your pocket."

Through Children's Minds

While there was no criticism of these advertisements for adults, to market similarly toward children could produce major public relations disaster and parental backlash, and this is discussed in a later chapter.

Through Children's Minds

Chapter 6

Maturing From Child to Adult Customer

While it is easy to conceive of a child as being a purchaser or influencing the purchase of a children's product such as a toy or game, considering them as the buyer of an adult product is more difficult since most adult products hold no significance for the child's mind.

Consider gasoline which many adults regularly purchase. How can a child's allegiance be gained for a product which holds no interest for them and they will be unable to purchase for many years? The answer is both simple and complex: by creating awareness of the product and an interest in it, and by involving the child in its use though for adult products this will necessarily reflect a distant association.

Why should a company bother to gain the interest of children in a product which they sell to adults? Because of the potential reward, as indicated by the following example.

Children do not often concern themselves with the brand of cold-cuts which is purchased for their family. But if a child's interest is gained through a figure or a game with which the brand is associated they may, as adults, be more likely to buy that brand since early life experiences are the bedrock of the mind.

Perhaps, as adults, they will make this purchase because they have come to prefer the taste of these cold cuts or associate the brand with quality. Or they may buy it out of nostalgia, their periodic desire to, symbolically, revisit their childhood through products associated with it.

If a four dollar package of cold-cuts is purchased weekly for fifty years by a million additional customers, the cost of the marketing to gain their allegiance will be insignificant. And, other factors being equal, how many parents would fail to purchase the X brand rather than the Y brand if their child requested it?

Awareness of a product or a brand can be made in ways which parents approve. An educational program can be created, as by having the brand or product become associated with a reading program; or book covers can be offered along with a contest for creating the best education slogan; or there can be a branded prize offered for the best student in some category. There might also be the sponsorship of a spelling contest, or the provision of information about communication or finance if the company's products involve these.

The key factor in this marketing is being subtle for the goal is to build a long-term allegiance, not to pressure parents for an immediate purchase.

It is crucial to gain parents' approval. Children may speak like adults, using similar words, but they are not adults. Lacking the insight of adults, children can be confused and deceived, and unwise marketing to children can be disastrous. This truism should be forefront in the minds of all who market to children.

Through Children's Minds

Chapter 7

The Child As Influencer of Family Purchases

Because of the high rate of divorce and single parenthood, and the rising number of families in which both parents work, the views of children and particularly of teenagers have become increasingly important in the marketplace. Restaurants seeking small customers with paying parents have long provided toys and packaged goods, while companies offer cartoon-character vitamins and specialty frozen meals.

To snare parents who want to vacation with their children while having time for adult activities, or to bring them on a business trip, hotels provide well-supervised day-care and cooking classes for children. But hopefully not dour teenage counselors, overcrowded facilities, and just large screen TVs or activities which children consider babyish or boring.

Parents seek places where the family is welcome and not just tolerated, which was the complaint of one parent at an expensive Manhattan restaurant: that families with children were placed as close as possible to the door. Still, other restaurants feel that the sight of a child conversing with a waiter contributes to the charm of the place.

The catalyst for change is money and businesses which do not change will lose customers. Parents today are older, have waited to have children, have more money, and want to enjoy activities with their children but in style too.

Whereas in the past a child would express the desire for a particular article of clothing and the nonworking spouse, usually the mother, would browse stores for the best buy, parents today are too tired after

Through Children's Minds

their workday. Now they are more likely to accept their child's advice about a purchase, the mother no longer being the all-powerful gatekeeper of the household.

Now, parents with less free time during the week seek quality time with their children over the weekend during shopping excursions, and marketers use the child as a conduit to their parents. Some brands are preferred by parents and their children grow up preferring them too.

Children *want* to buy for though they acquire their basic identity in their home, they also purchase elements of it in the marketplace. As youngsters gain shopping experience and parents yield spending decisions, marketers have taken aim at children though childhood interests are limited: one-third of their purchases are of snacks and sweets, another one-third of toys and games and crafts, and the rest consist of movies, sporting equipment, and clothing. But a child who buys a toy Black & Decker tool may well prefer that brand when they reach adulthood.

A small number of children purchase independently by the age of four, more than one-half by the age of six, and virtually all children buy independently by the age of nine. They develop early preferences about where to shop, preferring stores which are friendly to them (as by greeting them, providing smaller shopping carts, have low displays), and which their parents regard positively.

Marketers can relate to children in one of two ways: as the primary consumer, in which they buy objects; and as the secondary consumer, in which they influence the purchases of others (their parents, gifts from relatives). Parents have only so much disposable income and that goes toward their children first.

To be a primary consumer one needs money and

Through Children's Minds

children obtain this from gifts or by doing chores. The average weekly income increases from just under two dollars per week at four years of age to just under ten dollars per week at age twelve, with a bit over fifty percent of this being gained from allowance and the rest as gifts from parents or others (for birthdays and holidays; for excellent school grades; by working part-time for neighbors).

Research has found that children generally save about one-third of their income, half at home and half in a bank, and almost sixty percent of children between the age of nine and twelve years have bank accounts.

Some banks view children as representing an opportunity to develop a loyal, significant group of depositors for their total income is over eight billion dollars a year.

As children get older, the type of store where they prefer to shop changes. The youngest children (age four or five) prefer convenience stores, where shopping can be accomplished most easily, while those approaching the teenage years prefer specialty stores.

Psychologically, young children view "shopping" as relating to the supermarket, most likely because their earliest shopping experience occurred there. Shopping malls, large stores such as Walmart, and convenience stores are less significant in the young child's world-view of shopping.

Children are drawn to colorful aspects of the stores in which they shop. Though being somewhat uneasy because of the size and activity of shopping in stores, they generally consider shopping to be an exhilarating experience.

Children view themselves as both buying and influencing the purchase of goods ranging from food to toys to computers, with older children having the greatest

Through Children's Minds

influence. Nearly half of teenagers help to select the family car.

In one study, in eighty-three percent of the families, children were found to play a major role in restaurant decisions and half of the parents surveyed said that toy promotions affected their fast-food choices. If these findings are replicated and can be generalized across the population, restaurants might be well advised to spend most of their advertising budget on free toys and not prime-time television ads to adults.

Retailers have long used the same strategy: attracting children's attention with cute, flashy packaging and appealing to their parents by advertising the product's benefits.

The one market that companies can rely on is infants. Couples will buy the top-of-the-line products for their babies, the best diapers, baby wipes and skin care. "When you have babies, you're going to spend more," one parent said. "With your kids you just keep on giving."

Children become influenced by advertisements soon after the age of two years. Thereafter, they request the purchase of increasingly more products. By five years of age, about half of children understand that the nature of advertising is to persuade. Three years later, almost all children realize that ads are intended to get them to buy something.

By eight years, which is when children begin to relate more thoughtfully to their behavior, they begin to relate more maturely to products too. Then, they are able to consider more than one aspect of a product, and to use information which they gained to make a buying decision in a manner similar to adults.

By the time that children enter elementary school they have already learned an increasing number of phrases to use to persuade their parents ("Everyone has

Through Children's Minds

it!" "If I don't get it, I'll die!").

These appeals are learned from ads or from peers. A child may insist that a product will save their parent time or be essential for health or that it is educational. Several of these elements may be combined, as with the child's plea that a product will "make learning fun."

The human mind reacts to success and behavior which is found to be effective will be quickly adopted whether it involves having a tantrum or expressing compliments ("You're the *best* mother!").

Yielding to children's requests varies by product, it being greatest for child-related products (cereals, toys, games) and less for others (as pet food). When a child's request for an in-store purchase is denied, research has found that this led to conflict 65% of the time and unhappiness 48% of the time. The tendency for conflict and unhappiness is highest among 6-8 year olds but the conflict and the child's display of anger and sadness to their mother's refusal of purchase are short-lived. The mother's most common response is to repeat what she said.

Mothers generally agree to children's requests particularly as they get older, and the amount of conflict caused by requests is low. Older children ask less frequently, possibly because their mothers already know their desires and buy accordingly or because older children less often accompany their mothers on shopping trips. Most requests occur at home although those of younger children tend to be made while shopping with their mother.

Some children's purchase appeals are misunderstood and produce unnecessary conflict though the product may have great meaning and be important to the child's happiness. A prime example is the request for a toy gun, which often arouses a negative reaction from

Through Children's Minds

parents.

Children, both boys and girls, like to play with a toy gun because it reflects their developmental need. Still, this is forbidden in schools. In one expensive pre-school, children were forbidden to play with toy guns. So instead, they pointed their fingers and said "bang, bang."

Some authorities say that while not every child who plays with toy guns becomes a killer, every murderer *did* play with toy guns as a child. But, like many simplistic correlational conclusions, this argument is phony since all adult killers also wore diapers when they were infants.

Children are inadequate creatures and could not survive without the aid of adults. They often feel afraid and the need to protect themselves from the dangers which they believe that they confront.

A three-year-old boy was brought to my office for treatment. While he would do whatever his father wanted, the child ignored his mother's requests.

The boy described his daily nightmares. In one recurring dream, he was being eaten alive by wild animals. This child didn't realize that the danger he faced was psychological, inside of him which the dream symbolized, and not external. While we spoke, he chose two guns from among the toys in my office and wore them in holsters while he romped. A third toy gun he carried in his pocket. He felt that these could protect him from the dangers he confronted.

I advised this boy's parents to buy him a toy gun after explaining my reasoning. The father called me two days later. The family was going to a natural history museum. What should they do if their son saw the dinosaurs and became frightened? I advised that his son should be treated like a normal child. If he became frightened, he could speak with his parents or me about this.

Through Children's Minds

"How is he doing?" I asked the father a few days later.

"Very well," the father replied. "Now he does whatever his mother wants but he spends all day shooting people."

The toy gun which the parents bought for their son did not solve his problems. But it did reduce his anxiety so that he could function better.

Incidentally, the toy guns that I am speaking of do not shoot projectiles but merely make noise. Parents should be concerned about toy guns which project objects. Accidents, unintentional or not, can easily happen with children.

Not all children are affluent and most, except for the youngest, feel that they lack enough money. They can think of things which they would like to purchase but are unable to. Twenty percent of children have nearly half the income and, on average, spend twice as much as children their age. Their purchases tend to be of electronics and designer brand clothes. They also tend to be more involved in family decision making.

As with adults, the income of children is affected by the economy: inflation, a rise in prices, or recession. With rare exceptions, children are unable to increase the amount of money they receive and it may be decreased in times of family hardship with the sales of child oriented products being affected too.

Through Children's Minds

Chapter 8

The Global Children's Market

There is no mystery why American children's products should be marketed abroad since most of the world's population and three-quarters of its personal income is outside of the United States. Moreover, while the customs and consumer behavior in countries varies, the human psychology does not.

Though there are certainly national cultures there is also a children's culture. One in which play and snacks are central, and the reason given by children for buying one product and not another is often "because" or that a friend has it. Children are not exactly the same all over the world but they resemble each other closely and think differently from adults regardless of their nationality.

Children have childlike sensibilities and limitations, with fun and *intrinsic motivation*, the good feeling gained by successfully using one's abilities, being potent determiners of behavior, and influencing their parents' purchases too. And streets are no longer where children live but those with whom they interact electronically.

There are four things that television producers know go across borders: music, news, sports, and children. Other truisms is that while a joke in America might bomb in China since comedy is local, action is universal, and an attractive cartoon product will be enjoyed by all children.

Moreover, all children have the same basic concerns, to learn about life and how to behave, and there are nearly universal settings such as the park and the school and the store. But there is an art to getting the balance between your national and global markets, and

Through Children's Minds

one should not attempt to conquer the world in a single year.

If carefully done, some local themes can be exported. The basically American theme of a father being involved with their children was successfully exported to Japan though their image of the father has long been that of the hard working businessman.

Years ago, McDonald's ads successfully portrayed a striking theme (for Japan) of a doting father. In one commercial, a father rode a bike with his son perched on its back. While pedaling, the father spoke of how much he would enjoy eating a McDonald's meal at home with his son. In another ad, a father ended his play at a corporate ball game to eat the McDonald's French fry with which his daughter approached him. Another father decided to quiet his van load of screaming children by buying them McDonald's milk shakes.

To downplay the arrogant idea that foreign American values were being imposed, unknown, local actors and theme music from popular Japanese TV dramas were used in these commercials.

American sales techniques have also been exported as with Disney branded children's dishes being sold in Latin America using Avon Products army of door-to-door salespeople.

American manufacturers have long adapted foreign products for American tastes as evidenced by the popularization of salsa, a sauce loaded with diced tomatoes, though Mexicans consider the American product to be watered down.

Since toys are supposed to reflect reality it is logical that driving, which research has found to be the number one fantasy of American children, is being acted out using battery powered, miniature cars. These may also hold worldwide appeal.

Through Children's Minds

More than ninety percent of the world's population of families is outside of the U.S.A. and even in low-income countries, large amounts of money are spent on such children's items as snacks and play items. In Chinese urban areas the "4-2-1" indulgence factor has been cited, with four grandparents and two parents indulging one child. Some regard this excess as dangerous, feeling that a child who starts out spoiled finds that as an adult they can't get very far. But as I've told newspaper interviewers over the years, "You don't spoil someone by giving them what they want. You spoil them by depriving them of what they emotionally need."

In some countries there isn't the same array of toys and snacks as in the U.S.A. and competition for the children's market may be less competitive. Yet economic conditions for families can change rapidly, as when a country which subsidizes basic commodities decides to no longer do so, and Third World countries are still poor when compared to Europe and America.

There is also the factor that children are still learning what is culturally acceptable and are thus more open than adults to culturally different items.

Children in less developed countries may have greater education than their parents and introduce them to American products which they come to favor.

In developed countries it is expected that children will be dependent on their parents for gaining consumption related skills, knowledge, and attitudes, this dependency decreasing with the age of the child.

But this conclusion is not true with all immigrants to the United States or in developing countries where a reverse socialization may occur. There, even young children may be the major source of facts about the modern environment including information about consumption. But various factors affect the parent-child relationship, and the ability to accept information from children appears to be culturally determined.

One study found that while in the United States, children are perceived to be qualitatively different from adults, in some other societies children are considered as small adults. Another study found that Chinese children possess a social maturity commensurate with their physical capabilities and that their parents are less threatened by their children's independence. A lot is expected of Chinese children as they get older.

A study of an upper-middle class population of 8th grade male students and 88 mothers in India found that whereas American children learn about buying products from their parents, who were considered to "protect" their children from other sources of information, in India the children played a much more active role and were a valuable source of knowledge to their mother.

Indian mothers were more purchase oriented than their children, being more willing to buy new products, while their children related more to economic implications. Mothers also tended to process advertisement information less than their children, were guided more by brand name, and felt positively about advertising.

To plumb cultural differences, Western advertising companies have provided disposable cameras to children so they can take pictures of what they like and don't like instead of trying to explain it to a stranger. Researchers watch and listen as Chinese women clean their houses and talk about work and family. To increase comfort and acceptance, focus groups are placed in children's playrooms instead of offices.

While cultural differences in global marketing are important, it is important to keep in mind that before there is a geographic culture there is a children's culture.

Through Children's Minds

Children are very much alike around the industrialized world, loving to play most of all, loving to snack, and loving being children with other children. This makes viable having fairly standardized multinational marketing strategies to children around the globe.

What is universal is the child's desire for fun, and the likelihood of children using and demanding television marketed products which contain powerful, enjoyable fictive elements.

Television provides a new cultural background, a host of archetypes, identification and stereotype figures around which children can organize their imaginative experience, by wanting to be as beautiful as a doll or staging mock battles based on heroic space characters.

Watching television has given children the desire for a more active, mobile, urban lifestyle, and the expectation of a glamorous occupation. Though these effects can transcend culture, one need attune programs to the local culture and, of course, the quality of the production is important too.

The importance of cultural compatibility is reflected by what happened when a Spanish version of *Sesame Street* was tried in Mexico with half of each program being locally produced and containing characters, settings, and speech native to Central and South America though not specifically to Mexico. When the show was tested in Mexico City, children from very poor families learned from it as they did in the United States. But when tested in rural area, the show failed to achieve its learning goals since the rapid change of scenes and characters, which held the attention of city children, were distracting to rural children who were used to a slower rhythm of life.

A television program to teach reading in Niger in the 1960s was enormously successful though the children could not even speak the language of the school, which was French, and the school lacked trained teachers. Here, cultural compatibility was carefully considered in constructing the program.

Barbie's early life in Japan was not easy, with initial sales being second to Licca-chan, a half-French and half Japanese, fifth grade playmate with large, round eyes, black hair, Western dress, and a more natural figure than the blond, teenage Barbie. But Barbie later found success with a bigger face, rounder eyes, and changing tastes. Japanese teenagers began dyeing their hair as light as possible and Barbie was no longer considered American. In today's borderless era, Japanese children play with both Licca-chan and Barbie.

Chapter 9

Developmental Changes in Play

Toys are a huge and growing market with children getting more toys each year. Families are now smaller, parents are older, and children's expectations increase.

Few parents want to give fewer presents than the previous year even in hard times for when parents give gifts, they are also giving gifts to themselves, wanting to feel that their children are being treated in a special way.

More mixed-religion couples bring more families celebrating multiple holidays, and the high divorce rate means more split families creating competition to give gifts. Grandparents are living longer and giving more presents too.

Play is intrinsic to all children in all cultures as are many of their earliest toys such as dolls and pull toys. Psychologists believe that this early play enables the child to develop the rudimentary cognitive schemas which underpin their mental functioning. The child's powerful engagement with their toys indicates its genetically ingrained element. Through play, the child begins to grasp the nature of causal relationships, begins to plan and test concepts, and expands their ability to make judgments.

The use of toys in symbolic play relaxes a child. It removes them from the world of adult reality where they must constantly adapt to rules which they barely understand, permitting them entrance into a world in which reality adapts to *their* desires.

Through play the child can create, in an infantile manner, human role conflicts and master them. They can express their unconscious ideas and temporarily believe themselves to be the ruler of their universe, avoiding

Through Children's Minds

awareness of their distressing limitations.

While toys have a developmental allure for children, it is their other aspects which join this age level with that of teenagers in their love for toys. Toys can be powered by imagination, can protect us from our darkest fears and remind us of our vulnerabilities in an often mysterious world. The best movies, like the classic film, *Invasion of the Body Snatchers*, contain these characteristics but in a safe, well-tolerated manner. Just like the enormously successful ray gun toy which the Buck Rogers serial inspired.

This toy originated in a nineteen-twenty-eight, pulp magazine, short story in which an Air Force officer awakened from a coma in the twenty-fifth century into a world tyrannized by Mongolians.

Using the advanced weapons of that age which included rocket pistols, Buck, aided by his girl-friend, Wilma, and the scientist, Dr. Huer, battle to free the world from evil. This ancient mythical story and its modern twists produced lines of customers outside toy stores, all hungering for this Rocket Pistol to help their children feel safe.

Perhaps only children can experience true fun for only they can enter a fantasy land bounded by imagination, one unconstrained by adult codes and life's harsh realities.

While play was criticized by Western societies since medieval times, it being considered by religions and nations as interfering with acculturation into the serious business of work, this desire could not be completely suppressed. Play among adults was indulged through quilting parties and barn-raising and dances and musical entertainment, while play for children contained activities which would prepare them for military service or family duties. Only in the twentieth century was play

Through Children's Minds

finally considered acceptable for children, a nineteen-thirty White House Children's Charter having proclaimed "With the young child, his work is his play and his play is his work."

Yet, government declaration or not, children are intended to play from birth. An infant learns language by playing with sounds which he hears, and both child and caregiver play with each other, alternating the roles of player and playmate. As infants develop they play at being a spouse or a shopkeeper or a truck driver or a teacher or a police officer. In this way they gain separate identities and different senses of who they might be and prepare themselves to carry out these roles in adulthood.

Play tends to differ for boys and girls with the play of girls being more realistic, less fantastical about their future adult roles as if the separation between child and adult is less for girls than for boys. It may be too that, because of the decreasing number of two-parent families with many now being headed solely by women, boys are less familiar with their future roles as adults.

The play of both boys and girls contain times during which there is a loss of self-control through such behavior as twirling to cause dizziness, playing pranks, pushing others, and teasing. This is followed by a re-imposition of structure and order, as occurs in adult functioning.

There may be an optimum level of play equipment since it has been found that playgrounds with less equipment have more social games but also more social conflict (teasing, quarreling, hitting and crying), whereas with the presence of more equipment, the reverse occurred. Apparently, having too much equipment may interfere with social development too.

Over the past hundred years there has been a change in the recreation which boys and girls prefer so

Through Children's Minds

that girls have increasingly come to prefer what are typically considered "boy games," sports in particular, though with some sports, as football and wrestling, there has been little change and for reasons which every teenager understands. A teenage boy I knew, the member of a high school varsity wrestling team, voluntarily surrendered during an out-of-state match, refusing to compete with his female opponent.

Psychologists divide the play of children into four definite periods: Babyhood (from birth to three years); Childhood (from three to six years); Youth (from six to eleven years); and Adolescence (from twelve to nineteen years). Though this classification is helpful for research, the boundaries are not that simple for while chronological age is of greater influence than intelligence in the choice of play activity, the child's environment and emotional maturity factor into the equation.

During the first three months of life, the baby plays exclusively with their arms and legs, play with objects beginning thereafter. Their play is simple with much repetition and being largely imitative of what is observed in the environment. The favored toys for two-to-three-year-olds are mechanical, as cylinders which can be fitted into holes. Their play does not last for long, the median time for any one activity of three-year-olds being fifteen minutes.

While parents encourage cooperative behavior, the play of infants is naturally individualistic and self-centered and any attempt to change this will be resented. Only toward the end of the first year does the infant seek the companionship of others though their play remains solitary. The motivation for team play does not occur until the third year of life but even by the age of four, when the pleasure in companionship increases and interest in cooperative play predominates, children

Through Children's Minds

prefers to play as an individual.

During the earliest years there is no preference for the same or opposite sex playmates but this soon changes. Groups which form between three and five years of age are usually composed of both boys and girls with groups of one sex usually being of boys. Four-year-olds prefer playmates of their own sex but two-year-olds do not. This sex preference is unrelated to such factors as intelligence or height or extroversion or personal attractiveness for these have no influence on the groups formed.

While nearly all childhood play is colored by imagination, this predominates in kindergarten and the primary grades as the child tries to understand their world. Thus they pretend to be adults or animals, involved in family relationships or travel. Play demanding skilled movements is valued as children test their powers by running or jumping or hopping, with construction (blocks, sand, clay) and collecting beginning at three years and lasting until eight years. During early infancy the construction in unfocused; only after the age of three do the activities involve meaningful manipulation.

While some parents are disturbed by their child jumping from one activity to another, this is typical of the play of young children. The average attention span of the most popular play activities ranges from seven minutes for the two-year-old to just thirteen minutes for the five-year-old.

The major differences between the play of younger children and that of children who are between six to twelve years is the gradual increase in the number of team games engaged in and, especially among boys, strenuous outdoor play is most favored. Imaginative (make-believe) play gradually decreases after the age of eight or nine, and collecting decreases after the age of ten.

Competitive games, as opposed to simple running and chasing, become popular after the age of eight, and a "rage" for reading, particularly in girls, develops about the age of eleven. The reading interest of boys tends to be stories of adventure and mystery while girls' first interests are in stories of home and school life. By the high school years there is greater interest in adult themed than juvenile fiction.

About the age of ten, the tendency to socialize and play (athletics, card games) in "gangs" begins, reaching a climax between twelve and fourteen. Children tend to choose companions of the same intellectual level since dull children can't keep up with gang activities while gifted children become bored with them. Being a "good sport" and living close by or attending the same school are essential elements to membership in a gang.

Surprisingly, physical characteristics and intelligence (as evidenced by intelligence test scores) have small influence on who is chosen as the gang's leader

An important element in the type of play is the amount of space available. Children who live in crowded cities engage in play which demands little space, and rural children tend to collect many more objects than city children.

Despite the great interest in adolescence, there have been fewer studies of play during this period of development than of earlier years. Apart from video games, the most important form of play during adolescence is group play and athletic contests where strict rules and regulations govern the activity.

By early adolescence there has been a great decrease in the percentage of girls who play with dolls; and for both sexes in interests which are predominantly

Through Children's Minds

individual.

All games are broadly educational since they require children to play together and to follow rules, while competition ensures that games are interesting to play. Toy makers often pitch young children's toys as being developmental aids, with some suggesting that games for older children, such as puzzle solving or strategy games, promote analytic and problem solving skills and foster improved memory.

Through Children's Minds

Chapter 10

Child Psychology and Children's Products

Play is essential in a child's life, and is the natural work of a child. Toys are children's tools and a huge toy industry has arisen to create them. Far more than mere entertainment, toys enable a child's mind and brain to develop. Toys bridge the gap between a child's fantasy world and reality by stimulating the child's imagination which has not yet been burdened by reality.

Color and size and touch help a child to develop a correct view of the world, with some colors and shapes being more comfortable than others. Our eyes have been found to scan an image most quickly when its shape is a rectangle, the shape which is common to books and television screens.

According to a 2011 study of two-to-four-year olds, thirty-nine percent had already used a tablet or Smart Phone to play games or to watch videos, while twelve percent used a computer daily and twenty-four percent used a computer at least once a week.

The most helpful toys are relatively open-ended, capable of being played with in many ways. Thus the popularity of LEGOs, with its snap-together components which can be used and reused to create innumerable forms. Or, someday, a soft toy with enough computer power to really interact with a child, answering their questions and being the exceptional toy or a substitute friend for the isolated.

While some products are poorly conceived and even potentially dangerous, toys are as necessary to a child's healthy psychological development as is the social interaction with their parents. Rigorous psychological studies using metanalysis (the identification of patterns in several studies) of longitudinal (developmental studies, these being the best studies which psychologists conduct) have found that the presence of play materials and maternal involvement correlate strongly with cognitive development, and that the older the child, the stronger is this association.

In other words, the more the child plays and interacts with their mother (or parenting figure, who could be a man), the healthier will be the child's psychological development.

Play benefits both children and parents too. Playing with a child permits an adult to engage in activities which are good for them but which they would not otherwise do, and for the same reason that young children play: because it is fun!

Yet, psychologists have found that play provides more than just fun. Toddlers spend much time viewing and interacting with toys and other objects. These attract children because they draw them into action and serve as a source of skill development and tool mastery.

Studies have found that the more this activity occurs, the higher is the child's mental age beginning in the second year of their life with brighter children tending to choose more appropriate play materials to interact with.

Later, play materials serve as a focus of social encounters, gain social experiences for children and offer other opportunities for learning.

Toys such as dolls and action figures are useful in *pretend play,* which is no simple matter. There are individual tendencies to engage in pretend play with some children refusing to consider fanciful ideas while others embrace them no matter how outlandish they are.

Pretend play enables children to act out real world resentments, which parents believe is alright since it is

Through Children's Minds

only "pretend." This complex behavior varies on a continuum, at one end being linked to the capacity to deceive and lie, to "put on a show," whereas at the other end of the value scale is the engagement in religious ritual.

Adults feel enchanted but sometimes also uneasy when witnessing pretend play. Particularly if the make-believe play comes close to revealing real antagonisms, like the play of any angry child who creates a scenario in which parents die.

Yet the ability to symbolically create alternatives to reality, and to play with these realities, is deeply engrained in human consciousness and as important as our ability to create an accurate picture of the world in which we function. Thus, anticipating the future, does a young girl hold her doll and proudly proclaim, "I, a mommy."

Research has shown that having toys can both make little and a lot of difference to a child's psychological development for what matters is the type of toy.

There are three types of toys and their names describe them: toys of acquaintance, toys of stereotype, and toys of identity. Only toys of identity can make a tremendous difference in a child's life. These can vary greatly from a bicycle to a cuddly soft toy to a first-aid kit or a Barbie doll.

Despite the discomfort of some parents, the preference for "boy toys" or "girl toys" seems to be natural and divorced from social or cultural influences, despite the fact that in most cultures boys are more likely than girls to be encouraged to be tough and aggressive and competitive.

Biology seems to affect gender specific behavior. Studies have found that male infants tend to look longer at the videos of moving cars whereas girl babies look longer at the videos of moving faces. Moreover, toy cars and trucks make noise, unlike soft toys or dolls, and loud noises and commotion are key ingredients in many nonhuman primate dominance displays.

In a 2009 study of fetal testosterone, researchers measured hormone levels in the amniotic fluid of pregnant women and then studied their children for years after their birth. While testosterone levels were certainly higher in the male fetuses, female fetuses are exposed to some testosterone too and this was linked to their later preference for rough-and-tumble play, what is considered to be "male-typical" behavior.

A more recent study (2012) in Finland tracked the testosterone (T) levels in forty-eight newborns for six months and then tested the children's toy preferences when they were fourteen months old. Girls were more likely to play with toy trains if they had exhibited higher T levels as infants, and boys with lower T levels were more likely to play with dolls.

In several studies on nonhuman animals it was found that if the male hormone level in developing females was increased, they engaged in more male-typical play; and if the male hormone level in males was artificially reduced, they engaged in less male-typical play. Male monkeys showed a strong, consistent preference for wheeled toys rather than plush toys while the female monkeys showed no strong preference either way.

Thus, even though monkeys aren't exposed to cultural messages about what toys they should play with, they show sex-biased play patterns too.

While these findings would seem to make matters simpler for the toy marketer they do not for other findings add to the complexity of concluding whether there is a biologically determined, gender specific attraction to toys in humans.

Yet what may be important is not the toy but what the child does with it. If a girl is provided a space monster figure as a toy, she will tend to act out a drama or take it for a walk whereas the boy will tend to engage it in a war.

Other studies have found that while boys in Western societies have a strong preference for "boy toys," girls are not predisposed to reject them; and that the preference for a gender specific toy begins far earlier for boys than for girls, girls not preferring a "girl toy" until they are five whereas boys requested a "boy toy" beginning at the age of two. This stronger sex bias may derive from social and cultural pressure since boys receive more criticism for crossing the toy gender line.

There have been suggestions to counter the cultural pressure for gender specific toys based on the viewpoint that dolls encourage girls' interest in appearance while the boys' mechanical play hones those spatial skills which are key to success in engineering and the sciences. There is no reason why toys which cross gender boundaries cannot be created, such as doll houses filled with characters with technical professions and video games containing female characters who are Masters of the Universe.

There is a belief that the major difference between an "educational toy" and "a toy" is who it is marketed to, the former being marketed to parents as tools designed to increase their children's ability to function productively in school and adulthood while the latter are marketed to children and lack a formal educational component. In other words, whether the toy is marketed to gain the child's admission into an Ivy League college or to keep them quiet.

Until the age of six, girls use computers as much as

Through Children's Minds

boys and often demonstrate superior concentration and motor skills. But about the age of seven, when gender differences accelerate, the interests of girls changes. While boys are playing competitive games involving action figures, weapons, and crashing vehicles, girls' play tends toward storytelling, building careers, emulating heroines, and developing communities.

There is little opportunity for girls to act on their interests in current electronic games. While recent construction of these with feminine interest and story themes attempt to meet this product void, there is uncertainty whether girls play computer games less than boys because of the dearth of product or that it doesn't appeal to them. They hang-out with friends or go to the mall, preferring a social experience to the solitary or far more limited group experience of game play.

Video games with compelling personal stories, conflicts, and choices, would likely be of greater interest to girls, who certainly have the funds to purchase them. Children thirteen and under spend forty billion dollars annually while teenagers spend four times that.

Interestingly, Lara Croft, the heroine of the famous video game, *Tomb Raider*, reportedly began life as a man, her sex being changed when it was considered that she too greatly resembled Indiana Jones. Over time, Lara changed from a busty, daredevil pinup into a more realistic person, one who the average person could better relate to.

Though still possessing a model's looks, Lara, at first, looks nervous and feels overwhelmed, attempting to flee danger as a real-life person would. Yet this vulnerability, one which women find attractive in men, would likely not be welcomed in a male action figure and perhaps not continually in a female figure either.

Video games enable the player to learn skills which

Through Children's Minds

empower and grant the illusion of mastery, experiences which, eventually, Lara provides too. Yet, as this game ends, might not the female player experience regret for how quickly the real woman has been transformed into the artificial, cardboard hero of the video game medium. A Lara Croft who suffers while learning to flirt or from the anguish of dating violence might prove welcome.

In the quest for the ideal toy or game, the game creator must remain mindful that while too great frustration during play will discourage the player, too little frustration will discourage them more quickly. The goal of the game creator is to find that point where the two intersect for creation excites and encourages healthy cognitive development too.

Toy creation has expanded and in today's complicated media and marketing climate a toy is no longer a toy nor is a cartoon simply a cartoon. A child's idol, perhaps a popular live figure of a prime-time TV series, may become the basis for a cartoon show, a doll or a game, a line of clothing and accessories, a line of gadgets, stickers and other decorative items, a children's cereal, or the movie version. Toys become a TV series which originate more toys, with extended families of characters to accompany them on their adventures.

The universal idol for a child between six and twelve years is a male TV or movie star of any race; the second most likely idol originated as a fictitious creature from comic strips, a movie character, a toy, or a videogame. There is no child idol which exhibits truly broad, universal appeal to both sexes and major age groups (6-8 and 9-12).

Boys tend to prefer invincible, rough-and-tumble action figures who are on the right side of cataclysmic struggles between good and evil and always win. Younger boys prefer animated and fantasy figures whereas older

Through Children's Minds

boys are more apt to choose living male role models.

Girls tend to revere whimsical, cuddly, gentle creatures who require nurturing, or are fashion figures. Similarly to boys, older girls veer toward real people.

By the age of six, children tend to have outgrown the Disney characters they loved earlier though this interest is not suddenly extinguished but gradually lessens, they being unwilling to give up childhood and their childhood "friends."

Trademarked figures as Snap, Crackle, and Pop have little likeability since they have no lives outside of being emblems. They do not live on in achievements, battle evil, or have relatives and associates in continuing epics. Children are very conscious that these figures are advertisements. But whimsical trademark figures can play an important role in helping children to remember, recognize, and request specific brands.

Through Children's Minds

Chapter 11

The Art of Developing Children's Products

The most important principle to follow when creating a product for children is that you can't fool a child. Children know what they want and a children's product will not be successful, no matter the size of its advertising budget, unless it satisfies their important needs: meeting their feelings, and fulfilling their fantasies. The ultimate test for a children's product is the child and precisely what makes one toy a hit and another toy a flop remains elusive even if the toy isn't over-priced or at the end of a fad.

The toy market is hit-driven. Stores want what is "new" so toy manufacturers must introduce "new" every year. Electronic toys, like high-tech dolls, are vulnerable since the innovations on which these toys depend are constantly being refined. Moreover, children's perceptions of what is "fun" are fickle, like scary looking, floppy bugs which "should have been a hit" but weren't. And children like new products too, this being why the enormously successful Barbie doll is constantly having a new career and staying on top of trends and fashion.

Successful toys derive from their creator's intuition, as a clarifying idea that springs suddenly into mind. But these are not always correct. And for those who worship reports filled with numbers and disdain qualitative or attitudinal research, the comment by the late, famed Austrian-American psychologist and father of motivational research, Ernest Dichter, is still relevant: "ten thousand times nothing is still nothing!"

Successful toys sometimes derive from their creator's childhood memories. Finger-Flick arose from "finger-flick football": flicking a tightly folded paper triangle over a set of goalposts made by a friend's thumbs and index fingers. From this idea came a game board designed after a football stadium, with more complicated rules and the paper triangle being replaced with a colorful plastic ball.

Game cards as Pokémon, which capitalize on children's interest in collecting, have produced huge sales by pursuing the ready market in search of a product rather than producing a product in search of a market.

Some children's products are way outside the imagination of an adult: try putting a mouse in your mouth! One popular toy which appealed to children's peculiar sense of humor and desire to horrify was the Half Rat Snack: a soft, gray, rubber device that you dangle outside your mouth. For extra verisimilitude there was a tongue-activated switch that wiggled the rat's tail.

And if this doesn't appeal to your appetite, perhaps you will like the Heart Ball. When squeezed, it makes "oozing and sloshing noises only a coroner could stomach," or the Micro Mucus since "It's snot what you think." "That's disgusting" is high praise as a child's reaction to a toy.

While these products may appear unworthy of serious effort, they were popular and met experienced needs. Children are the customers of tomorrow and holding the false attitude that they cannot discriminate between products which are good or poor will doom the present and the future of the best intentioned company.

For companies which have long been child oriented like toy and snack companies, their efforts will merely extend what they have already been doing: producing largely the same product for an older or younger audience. For other companies, children will present a new market which needs to be addressed through advertising or children's clubs or events. Either

Through Children's Minds

way there is financial risk though this will be greater if new products are sought rather than creating a small product extension.

While it will be less costly to make the children's product a mere extension of the adult product, this effort almost always fails for it violates a basic creed of modern psychology: that children think differently from adults. A me-too product may be considered "boring" by children, and be regarded as an unnecessary expense by parents.

A designer who seeks to please only themselves will likely wind up with a product only they will buy, and this is particularly true of products intended for young children. Before learning adult cultural mores, children are children and attracted by the child motives of curiosity and fun. They seek objects which allow them to be playful.

Yet successful children's toys can be extensions of adult objects, as with miniature cars and trucks and make-up kits. The very low price of micro-toys allow children to buy these miniatures with their allowances, and appeal to children who are fascinated with collecting. Many of these toys come as multi-part series and are portable, having their own small carrying cases that can hold numerous little pieces.

These small toys are an example of how less can be more though their tiny size present a danger to children younger than four who tend to put things in their mouth. Ethics, regulatory oversight, and a company's business reputation demand that a company's warning of a toy's inappropriateness be in the clearest fashion.

The toy may be specific to children, like a small bus containing an electronic number learning game or a bear which plays a song when a large button is pressed. Or, of greatest attraction, a toy which seems alive and is a child's dream come true. A recent attempt is the one-

Through Children's Minds

hundred dollar WowWow RoboMe, a foot-tall customizable, iPhone-based robot toy. Through its app, the child can choose eye shape, facial hair style, and accent. RoboMe also has voice-recognition software and an infrared sensor so it can learn voice commands and avoid obstacles.

While toys are show business and a toy that looks great on television may soon lose its novelty, the child may continue to use it in their imaginative play.

Some companies target their toy marketing to parents, as for the attractive, soft, cuddly mother doll who comes with a small baby and bottle. She isn't as shapely as Barbie for this doll is intended to be purchased by mothers who consider Barbie just another bimbo.

Mere simplicity cannot guarantee that a children's product will be successful for it must also satisfy the important psychological need of providing *intrinsic motivation*. Activities which are performed for their own sake are described as being *intrinsically motivated*, that is, there is pleasure experienced in the activity itself.

Play is intrinsically motivated. Everyone, including children, develop mental pictures, psychological structures of their world. Psychologists believe that intrinsic motivation results when a child encounters a stimulus which does not match their existing cognitive structure. This produces conflict and discomfort which the child seeks to reduce through the natural activation of curiosity, exploration, and playfulness, with objects of greater novelty and complexity being preferred.

Though both exploration and play are used to reduce this cognitive discomfort, they are different. Exploration is more focused and less joyful than play, more geared to discovering the characteristics of an unfamiliar object. Play is more relaxed and involves the child's makeover of the object, which occurs more readily with familiar objects.

Play provides intrinsic reward by enabling a child to gain a sense of competence, of mastery over their environment. But play may also be engaged in to gain the approval of peers or for competition, during which the intrinsic motivation is lower.

The basic human survival needs, shelter and food and health care, are provided for children by their parents and, except occasionally with food, children have little choice. But for other activities, those which occupy most of their free time, children may be considered the consumer. And what satisfies one of their crucial needs are objects which satisfy their need to play, and provide them with the joy of intrinsic motivation.

While the concept of play is usually applied to toys, it is relevant to a large number of products. Food or clothing can gain a playful element by associating them with a licensed character. Even I, who am well into adulthood, was entranced by the sight of a hooded Star Wars jacket. It had a hidden wire leading into its pocket which, when pressed, caused the symbol affixed to the jacket to glow. *"That jacket is really something,"* I said, admiringly to the adult wearing it.

The concept behind that jacket is no different from that of the glowing sneakers worn by many young children though no teenager or adult will wear these. Both garments grant an element of playfulness to ordinary clothing, and at comparatively small cost.

Transformer toys, in which parts of a figure can be assembled in different ways, are not only playful but enable a child to experience their desired sense of mastery. It is both of these elements which have caused their popularity, as well as the long popularity of model car and airplane kits. Perhaps fast-food restaurants, to increase their appeal to children other than by providing small toys, should offer children the opportunity to complete their meal by adding healthy but tasty additions made of wheat germ or soy or non-fat milk. This would likely be welcomed by parents even if each addition were associated with a particular rank of space warrior.

But this idea is mine, that of an adult. Whether these additions would be considered playful, and thus desirable to children, can only be determined by conducting research with children, not by asking adults whether it seems worth doing.

But whether a product attracts children is not the most important part of the sales equation since the reaction of parents is more important. If parents, or retailers, believe that a product is dangerous, not only will it not sell but its production can devastate a company's image in addition to raising the possibility of expensive liability. The younger the children for whom the product is intended, the greater will be the parental veto power over its purchase.

The product's package should be given close attention. Is it colorful enough to attract children and small enough for their hands? Are the instructions clear, in language which matches the cognitive level of the intended customer? Asking children to read and interpret the directions might prove an eye-opener.

When creating children's products, having a good idea is far from enough to assure success.

Advertisers and marketers attempt what Walt Disney termed *imagineering*: the engineering of imagination. He tried to combine the power of his animation technique with the romance of his characters to enthrall the viewer's imagination. Because the earliest audience for his cartoons were children, he used techniques which are naturally comical to children and have since become common: exaggerated bodily

Through Children's Minds

movements and limbs and eyeballs; impossible events such as figures crashing through walls yet surviving; animals becoming airplanes; rubbery objects becoming rigid and vice versa; and, of course, falling over a banana skin.

Still, the plot followed the storyline of previously successful films in which common events went awry. Movie directors have created numerous successful thriller movies with the theme of a normal person's usual day turning deadly.

Disney's characters were often innocent but endured suffering because of their understandable mistakes and through the misunderstanding of others. Anything that could happen might happen and often did. These animated characters lived in an unstable world and followed assumptions which proved unfounded. This is the same life as that of the inadequate every-child who lives in a world controlled and managed by adults.

This is why, on an unconscious level, children can identify with the lives of Disney characters and enjoy Disney animations. They present the world of fictional characters but it is also their world.

Yet the world of Disney's imagery and mythology, as presented in his full-length movies beginning with *Snow White*, presented a world which adults could appreciate too. A society of innocence and justice and community and the triumph of goodness, themes which have been woven into the most popular American films.

The Disney characters' popularity with children increased the significance of the licensed goods industry. The Disney Company's later efforts, as with their televised *Mickey Mouse Club* and its millions of daily child viewers, showed the power of enabling a sense of tribal belonging which marketers exploit today.

Another element which later producers followed

Through Children's Minds

was the children's preference for comedy, with the violence being in a form which parents couldn't object to since the characters were unreal and their actions were wacky.

In both cartoons and children's stories, problems were resolved, either in some never-never land or real life, often with the intervention of a creature with almost magical powers. Which is what children consider their parents to possess.

Successful toys will be capable of modification depending on the age of the child. There is a great change in the capacities of children as they develop and a toy should hold an increasing challenge which a child of increased capacities can also enjoy. Perhaps the great success of LEGO is that it was conceived not as a toy but as a system of play.

To provide "intrinsic play value and ingenuity" was the founding belief of Fisher-Price eighty years ago and it would be hard for a toy company to improve on this motto. Incidentally, Fisher-Price firmly believes in research and refines toys in its nursery school laboratory.

Toys that both preoccupy and educate children are most desired by parents but these should also make children happy and contented.

Successful toys are not mere playthings but are invested with fantasy and a story line. If a figure, the creature should have a personality and a life. If a construction, the toy should be part of a universe of activity, essential for the successful assembly of a figure or society.

The toy's fantasy should be capable of meshing with the child's imagination to create new story lines, ones which will be inherently more vivid since they are self-created and unique.

Many business products are created with the

Through Children's Minds

concept that all people see things the same way, that the same culture and values are shared by manufacturer and customer. But adults and children have different cultures and values, and children seek to use a product in their own individual way.

Thus, girl software should be girlish, containing introspection and dreamy fantasy with classmates who share advice as they become enveloped in hungered for but anxiety-laden romance.

Nerve-wracking conversations with boys can be replayed with different girlish responses, teaching that kindness and charm work more effectively than aggression. There can be such problems as "my dream date is a lousy kisser" to cope with.

These issues follow the ancient themes of the female gothic novel and are experienced most vividly during adolescence: friendship, sexual threat, and betrayal.

Being creative is part art and part science, thinking both rationally and emotionally. Creativity involves the basic human processes of imagination, expression, and association. The problem, a creative challenge, produces conflict because of apparent limits and inconsistencies. The creative attempt breeds tension and passion until an integrative resolution is achieved with a new, exhilarating state of association and meaning being realized. The creative process consists of the successful resolution of what had seemed impossible through the management of opposing forces.

Once you have decided on an approach, let yourself go emotionally in order to tap your unconscious, creative reserve and make it work for you. This is the kind of primitive, symbolic process that we are trained to avoid though most creative business decisions are instinctive, based as much on intuition as facts.

Through Children's Minds

Using creative judgment is an ill-defined, nebulous quality which must be developed and being unafraid to ask what might be considered dumb questions is a start.

Creating a product of novelty and value requires a shared social construction between the producer and the receiver on an unconscious level. The natural unity of intuition, thoughts, and feelings motivates people to transform their ideas into realities and to demonstrate their ideas as realities. Much like the oriental principle of Yin and Yang, which views life as a rhythmic harmony of paired opposites within a timeless movement of interpenetrating enigmatic patterns.

Through the intuitive process, "hard" product thinking interacts with the "soft" thinking of play and challenge and chaos, with each evolving and sustaining the other.

Through Children's Minds

Chapter 12

The Uniqueness of Marketing to Children

To successfully market to children means that we must think as they do, to ruminate logically but also quirkily. To avoid trying to see a pattern where there is none, to being unafraid to be wrong, to accept that children, like adults, do not always behave rationally. And, most importantly of all, to look for the magic in a product and to create magic in the way that it is sold.

Children love to be amazed and creating magic is a key part of successfully marketing to them. This magic can be technological, as with a more capable electronic doll, or in the service arena by having a special area for children at the supermarket. Perhaps one with free snacks and populated by a toy parrot which electronically repeats anything said into its mouthpiece or even a live parrot if the regulatory code for food establishments permit this.

The youth subculture is a distinct, cohesive lifestyle with shared interests, language, rituals, and idols. Marketers to the youth market create special symbols or situations, and use peer group persuasion to spread the advertising message.

The Walt Disney Company found great success in establishing a peer group with its creation of the televised *Mickey Mouse Club* in the 1950s.

Peer pressure to use the "right" object exists with children and teenagers to a degree which is not present with adults. And advertising can "arm" children in their negotiation with parents though children are not innocent about its aim. By the age of five, half of all children understand that advertising is intended to persuade, and by the age of eight, almost all children realize that advertising is intended to get them to buy something.

For many adults, shopping is a necessity and best accomplished as quickly as possible. Their free time is limited and they have other responsibilities, interests, and enjoyments. Even if, when feeling down, a person can lift their mood by buying themselves a present though this does not change their life.

Adults have made daily purchases for decades so their enthusiasm for shopping can be difficult to arouse. They may pick among items in which all brands are considered equally good with the purchase being based on a whim or at random.

But *choosing a product* involves making a decision based on a preference which may be rational ("I'm buying this brand because it was dependable in the past.') or only partly rational ("I can identify with the person in the ad."). Consideration may be given to the opinion of a spouse or the desire for variety and so the ordinarily purchased brand is ignored. This deliberation may not be completely logical for the person's reasoning may be faulty and affected by wishful thinking or emotion.

Shopping by children is less complex for it is both an adventure and an activity to be learned. If an adult were to be asked why they were entering a store, they might well consider the questioner to be crazy for everyone knows that people enter stores in order to shop. But just as the filling-up of a car at a gas station seems mysterious the first time that teenagers do it, so too must the nature of shopping be learned. A connection must be made between the store and the television ads and the ability to satisfy one's needs. This knowledge begins to be gained in the second year of life though it is so ingrained in adults that they cannot remember ever having had to learn it.

Through Children's Minds

Months later, between the age of two and three years, other essential experiences are gained. Children begin to make requests of parents and to try out elements of the consumer role which include the sense of products having brands and that one product is "better" than another. The child also learns that a certain type of goods can be obtained in a certain type of store.

Between the age of three and four years, children begin selecting products on their own, and developing store preferences depending on their comfort level with particular stores. Parents encourage product selection, using this opportunity to educate their child about desirable consumer behavior.

Beginning at five and on through the teenage years, children make independent purchases and become increasingly able to satisfy their needs by becoming more skillful as a shopper. By age six, the child has formed many of their buying habits and these will remain throughout their life.

Yet even teenagers are less sophisticated shoppers than adults for adults have a greater capacity to relate their needs to what is available, and can relate with greater objectivity to the shopping experience.

Apart from their youthful limitations, there are other reasons why it is more difficult to market products to children than to adults. Since there is no large body of marketing experience for children as there is for adults, each element, from product to packaging, must be researched anew. Is the packaging attractive to children? Can they reach it on the shelf? Can a child understand the instructions for the product's use? Can they open the package? Can they remember the brand name, considering that it's almost impossible for a young child to remember products whose names contain three or more words?

Through Children's Minds

Moreover, the emotional and personality structures of children differ from those of adults. In a major study, among the questions asked of twelve hundred children, age six to seventeen years, was, 'Do you wish your family were bigger?" Some of these children replied, "No, my family is plenty tall.' And in another study, while adult marketers had believed that the biggest worry of children was war, the children stated that their number one worry was a bad report card.

Marketing to children can also involve one in difficult legal, legislative, and ethical situations. Too often, headlines blare such news as "FTC Hits _____ Agency For Ads", "In Settlement, Toy Maker To Give Refunds," these complaints being about toys which were advertised to do things which they could not, and a manufacturer having failed to disclose that assembly was required.

Sometimes the marketer can't win even if a product sells outrageously well. After a spate of robberies of teenagers for their highly priced, athlete endorsed sneakers, a columnist likened the endorsers to drug dealers ("They're both working off a copy of the same marketing plan. Why isn't every one of them screaming for these kids to stop killing each other? Because they've sold their names to the sneaker and apparel manufacturers or they're taking ad money.")

The language of ads intended for children has also been criticized ("What are TV ads selling to children? 'Ain't life delicious'–they don't only sell candy, they sell language!")

An exhaustive study of network programming concluded that "sinister combat violence" pervades a significant number of Saturday morning children's cartoons, that the cartoons were least likely to show the long-term effects of violence, and that violence was frequently (67%) portrayed in a humorous context. This, though children realize that the violence on a TV show is fictional and relate to it differently than if they were to read the same scene in a book. Public opinion does not always follow the findings of research.

While such marketing behavior will elicit few if any complaints from youth, the marketer must be continually concerned with the reactions of parents and other adult customers. A person buying for a company, to avoid offending co-workers, will avoid purchasing the products of a company which is tainted by scandal.

There is also the pain experienced when a marketer engages in conduct which violates their conscience by conflicting with their values and self-image. And, of course, the powerful sanctions which are available to government authorities.

Another significant difference between the adult and child customer is that disappointing a child customer can cause far greater future loss of sales than disappointing an adult customer. Children will someday be major purchasers for themselves, their family, and their grandchildren, and will influence their friends and relatives. In one study, sixty-two percent of college students and fifty-six percent of college seniors were found to buy the same brand of toothpaste they used during high school. Children lack the flexibility of vision and knowledge which can enable an adult to excuse a marketing or product error.

There are other differences too. The adult has greater independence of behavior than the child. Children shop where their parents or other adults take them or where they can go by themselves, and where both they and their parents feel comfortable. Stores marketing to young children will be more successful if they have toddler-height counters and low handrails. Older

Through Children's Minds

children would appreciate a free club membership and newsletter.

The adult also has greater knowledge of advertising and marketing than the child though the child's awareness of advertising and marketing advance as they mature.

The adult purchases and is interested in buying a wider range of objects than the child. But while historically, marketing to children was confined to toys, candy, snacks, and cereal products, children influence the purchase of a far wider range of products than these.

The adult has had far more shopping experiences and possesses a greater number of beliefs about products and business names and trademarks than a child. But children are very brand conscious. One child, when expressing their preference for a widely advertised brand of frozen pizza over a less expensive store brand, stated, "Any store-brand thing is gross."

The purchasing undercurrents are different for an adult than for a child, and they relate to media differently, as is described in later chapters.

Finally, children do not share the same cultural values as adults. No adult would purchase a "gross" object yet for children *gross* is a hot item.

But one characteristic which is shared by both children and adults is the desire to have fun, and this is why Halloween has become the second biggest holiday in the country. Modern America has become more non-institutional and casual so non-religious holidays like Halloween are perfect for us. It is an intergenerational holiday that appeals to everyone and can be celebrated by the young, by the old, and by fast-food and snack manufacturers with their spooky creations.

Now, a few words about marketing to teenagers. While using current offhand phraseology is OK between

Through Children's Minds

teenagers, the advertiser must be careful not to talk down to them for this will be regarded as phony and condescending. Sincerity is better than cuteness and having only an attention getting approach often dissuades teenagers from a product. Emphasize the value of the product since teenagers like to be credited for making rational decisions and are quick to notice a change in price or value.

Be as personal as possible since a prime developmental task for adolescents is the development of a sturdy sense of who they are.

And, as should be true of all advertisements, be scrupulously honest. For example, showing teenagers in a car with their parents and not fighting is too perfect. Or, more usually, the fighting is obviously fake.

Finally, advertisements must strike the right tone with a wide range of ages. A gritty commercial may delight teenagers but frighten younger children.

Just like children, children's advertisers play hide-and-seek too. They place ads in movies, causing some to resemble billboards on film with all the brand-name products they include. Perhaps because, unlike television which is regulated by the Federal Communications Commission, films don't face restrictions due to constitutional free-speech protection.

Through Children's Minds

Chapter 13

What You Must Know
To Create New Marketing Ideas

A young child summed up the problem which children's product marketers continuously confront: "I like lots of stuff and I just don't know what I really want," the child said, during a visit to New York's FAO Schwarz' one-hundred-fifty year old New York City flagship toy store.

While food, water, clothing, and shelter are the only life essentials, it is the nonessential products which add richness to life. A life without social companionship or books or drama is impossible to grasp for these feed our feelings and our development as humans.

Because some of our motives are unconscious, and particularly those which provoke behavior until a person is well into their adolescence, it is important to understand the role of the unconscious in purchasing. Not to seduce a child into buying something which will fail to fulfill their need but in creating products which will better fulfill them. In other words, to give the buyer, whether child or teenager, more exactly what they want. These, for the young consumer, are objects which satisfy their need to play.

There are several general rules in marketing to children but the most important is that no general rules apply. There is no reason to assume that a specific segment of children are appropriate for your products. So while market segmentation is good in moderation, your target should be well-defined and large enough to make economic sense. American teenagers have great discretionary income and freedom but they also have a unique life style in many ways.

Through Children's Minds

Children, for the purposes of marketing, may be considered to range from three years of age, which is the first year of consumer activity, until eighteen years, which is the last year of high school. But factors besides age such as race and ethnicity may be important too though minorities should never be regarded as one market. The Hispanic segment is made up of several heterogeneous groups.

Differences among ethnic groups are small among younger children but become significant at the onset of the teenage years because adolescence is the stage at which people form ethnic and cultural identities.

As children grow older, the range of products they buy with their own money expands constantly. Significant spending on products which are not traditionally considered "children's products" begin in the 9-11 year age group. While much of this group's spending is still devoted to snacks and toys, they also spend a lot on fast food and entertainment and this increases greatly during the teenage years.

For girls age 9-11, grooming products such as deodorant and hair products become important and girls are typically introduced to brands of these products by their mothers, there being little experimentation after that.

Teenagers fear that switching shampoo, medication, or antiperspirant/deodorant brands would jeopardize their appearance or social acceptability and feminine-hygiene products enjoy the greatest loyalty among teenagers.

Even the demographic term which one uses when describing adolescents is important since older teenagers feel that the word "teen" indicates someone younger than them whereas younger teenagers (12 to 15 year olds) embrace the term.

Through Children's Minds

While parents spend far more on children's products than do children for all age groups, both spending and purchase influence grow as children get older. Influence grows faster than spending among younger children, while spending grows faster among teens.

While advertising is used to symbolize a product to both children and adults, communicating with children is very different from communicating with adults. Children find abstract concepts hard to understand and even more difficult to express, and their response to ads is to those which are more emotional and visual and less dominated by language.

Because children have difficulty remembering the characteristics of products, they tend to relate to advertisements which have "kid appeal" and are repeated. They prefer products based on brand image and the perceived social standing of products among their peers. Thus, commercials for children should place heavy emphasis on social information and not merely the characteristics of the product.

Children do not make rational judgments about a product, that is, view it as being the way to satisfy their experienced need. Because of their limited communication abilities, their preference for non-verbal communication, and their inadequately developed sense of who they are, the issue of having the "right" toys is a matter of great importance and emotional intensity for them. They like things that are uniquely their own.

Children communicate through objects, with products that help to integrate their identity and to identify with their peers. Advertisers must be sensitive to the changing flux of children's social symbols and learn to convey these symbols effectively.

Because play is often a social activity in which the

toy orchestrates the behavior of two or more children, peer influence is one of the most important aspects of product requests in the toy market, and the social judgment of peers plays a crucial role in a child's liking for a product.

Children learn most about new toys from television advertising and their friends. In one study, more than three-quarters of the toys which children wanted were first introduced to them in television commercials.

Watching children at play appeals to them and peer power is the root of the strategies in television advertising. Here, children have the sense of being surrounded by others who share their judgments about products.

While children see themselves as being part of an age stratum, it is not adequate to use just any peer in ads. Children are harshly judgmental of children in ads who violate subtle peer expectations and exhibit improper style. Young girls prefer identifying with and like models who are slightly older than themselves.

Children also have clear ideas about gender differences: boys react badly when girls appear in ads for "their" products, while girls react badly to the presence of boys to a lesser extent. Not recognizing their implicit assumptions about peer could jeopardize the success of a product.

Personality promotes loyalty to a product line because personalities are easily remembered and therefore bypass the young child's inability to remember the characteristics of products. Personality also provides the means of emotionally involving children in the product and enables children to communicate easily to their parents what they want without having to know the brand or corporate name.

In order to promote character toys, one must grasp

Through Children's Minds

the nature of children's identification with heroes and role models. But this is not simple and explains why many properties fail. Research is needed in the early stages of character development and licensing to identify which new figures have or do not have potential and to identify which segments of the children's market are most likely to accept the new character. No character will be universally accepted by all ages and with both genders. Early, small research spending can protect later, large investments in product and media.

Children are fussy about their toys and there is a segregation in character preferences along age and gender lines. As was earlier stated, boys prefer invulnerable figures who win their battle for justice. Girls prefer gentle creatures they can nurture, or fashion figures if they have begun to veer towards their romantic inclinations. Children under six prefer cartoon characters.

It is important not to overly specify a doll since this would limit the imagination of the child playing with it. Yet leaving too much of the doll's personality and life for the child to specify can also inhibit its appeal for this would demand too much of the child's imagination. Providing some but not too many facts about the life of the character is the key here.

The successful toy must be properly positioned and situated within the everyday experience of children's lives, created to be unique in relation to other products in the same niche. The product must be defined in the child's mind through links to emotions and activities which they value.

A product can be defined through show and tell, personification, and plot pivots. Also through association by connecting the product to admired people and celebrities and familiar associations. These associations work because children familiarize themselves with products on an emotional level.

Communicating the benefits of a product is least effective because of the limited communication ability of children. Marketers should test for whether children latch onto a distinct identity for the product and make a positive association with it, not whether they understand the concept of the ad or even whether they fully understand the story.

Marketers tend to draw inappropriate carryovers from models of adult consumer behavior. These can make it difficult for them to see the holistic nature of children's thought. When concerned with children, one must downplay the term *decision* and stress an *orientation* model instead.

Children, as consumers, don't make rational choices about products. Rather, they move through life following one orientation after another. Their involvement with the marketplace is characterized by a global, undifferentiated manner of approaching things. For most children most of the time, liking and knowing are part of the same global response. The problem for the marketer is how to orientate the child towards their product, which can be done through definition, association, or proposition. To sense what children orientate toward, we must first understand the complexities of their emotional life.

For a child, the ideal doll is a personality with possibilities: a vision of the child's life *as it can be* which enables children free rein with their fantasies and on which they can prop their private dreams.

One hundred years ago, Sigmund Freud described the *repetition compulsion* whereby people endlessly repeat a situation or a pattern of behavior which was difficult or distressing in their earlier life. By doing this

Through Children's Minds

they attempt to master the situation.

Repetition is one of the two basic principles followed by all marketers. The second is to appeal to the emotions of the consumer.

When children play, they repeat what has made a great impression on them. And because there is no repetition, or imitation, without an emotional component, companies battle to have their trademarked goods placed with well-loved figures and in movies.

Adults like to think of childhood as being a carefree, happy period but frustration and fear are frequent. To emotionally embrace their illusion, adults buy Winnie-the-Pooh or Mickey Mouse products in business books and golf-club covers and silk ties and kitchen towels, feeling nostalgic for a safer world where nothing too terrible happens. Or they fret about the spread of germs among young children and purchase more expensive, germ resistant toys which have an antibacterial chemical incorporated into the plastic.

A five-year-old girl who is about to begin school may play at being a teacher to the delight of her parents, but her behavior might really reflect her fear of the unknown teacher's authority and what could happen in class. Thus, through play, the girl reduces her anxiety by jumping the gulf between wishing and being.

Similarly, a child may choose an inanimate object, a doll or toy animal or even a pillow, to assume a role which will change the child's status into a parent or a sibling or even a dog. Through this seemingly casual play, the child retaliates for the things they have experienced or gains experiences which they wish, and these desires motivate such play.

That toys should be safe goes without saying but children can play with things in ways which the manufacturer never intended. Some years ago a much

Through Children's Minds

loved, plastic carrot and French fries chomping doll was found to chomp on children's flowing hair which became snarled in gears in the doll's throat. Many complaints were made to the Consumer Product Safety Commission.

Play can enable a child to cope with their fears, as when they pretend to be a monster in order to help them walk into a dark room where they fear that a monster lurks. Play can also help a child to reduce their anger towards those whom they feel, justifiably or not, that it would be dangerous to express angry feelings towards. Thus a wall is destroyed in fantasy with a toy gun, or a construction is smashed.

Play enables children to experience pleasures which maturity has forced them to give up. By pretending to be a baby, a child can permit themselves to suck their thumb or to talk babyish and thus relax within the less constrained world of babyhood. Or a child can immerse themselves within the amoral world of a cartoon character who exhibits disobedience or greed, behaviors which would cause then to feel guilt or shame or gain punishment were they to behave similarly.

Play can change a sad ending into a happy one, as by recreating an experience at an amusement park where a parent refused an activity.

Some believe that the younger the child, the briefer is their span of attention. But this is only true when the child is provided something which is suitable for someone older. The play of young children, even when they are with others, resembles more a dream than a drama. Characters and roles come and go in ways that make little sense to the observer though the play completely satisfies the participants.

Children may repeat behavior nearly endlessly without apparent reason. But even the simplest repetition has value for by repeating an experience the child divests it of its uniqueness and the discomfort which novelty arouses even in adults

Much children's play is the test action by a creature who lacks the adult capacity for symbolic thinking. Through play the child can try-on different roles; and help themselves cope with anxiety before a feared event and to deal with the anxiety afterward.

Despite the difference between play and thinking in the amount of energy expended, they share important similarities. Playful repetition is an indispensable first step towards the ability to think, a capacity which is limited in young children. Both thinking and play deal with real elements which can be varied. Both thoughts and play behavior can change quickly, and both require imagination. And, through repetition, unsatisfactory elements of play and thinking can be reworked, to be more successful the next time.

Certain characteristics are present in all children's play: physical movements, fun, and humor. These three elements will be present in the creation of an ideal children's products.

For educational products and for software programs intended for young children, product designers should follow the example of *Sesame Street* and emphasize animation, puppets, and sound effects. They should also follow the advice of the great developmental psychologist, Jean Piaget, that to learn something new you generally have to be able to relate it to something you already know. Thus, to teach a letter shape you would start with a familiar object having the same shape as the letter being taught.

Other important points to remember when creating educational products are: (1) that repetition enhances learning; (2) to make the child an active participant; (3) to enable the child to manipulate and

Through Children's Minds

control the content; (4) to have icons and picture menus to navigate; (5) to enable the child to gain help and change activities independently; and (6) to provide the child with feedback about their accuracy and progress.

The parent should receive information on the developmental appropriateness of the program's content and how to extend its learning activities to off-computer learning experiences. If children can't seem to grasp the cause-and-effect relationship of moving the mouse on the table and seeing the character move around the screen, they're probably too young for the program.

Very young children find tablets like the iPad easy to master and can swipe with their fingers as well as their parents, I heard of one two-year-old who, by herself, phones her father long distance via Skype and I'm sure that there are others.

Electronic devices can be valuable to young children for it is crucial that they become acquainted with books. Gadgets attract children even more than they do adults and a parent who reads together with their child from a Kindle or an iPad or a Nook will greatly increase the probability of their child's future academic success.

Just as the mind is genetically programmed to deduce the grammatical structure of language it can, naturally, enable the child to read before beginning kindergarten, but only if they earlier become acquainted with books. Reading on a touchscreen adds to the child's enjoyment and has the additional effect of increasing their sense of mastery over the environment.

Unfortunately, much educational software should be termed "edutainment" for it is not really educational. Instead, it promotes passivity and dull creativity and arouses concern about the children's future ability to reason well and to communicate effectively. Words are taught as isolated objects, lacking real meaning, and many children randomly click on words until they find the right one or memorize the story to make it seem as if they are reading.

A study in 2013 by the Pew Research Center found that most teachers thought that the use of technology, from tablet devices to Google Docs, encourage collaboration among students and creativity and personal expression, in middle and high schools. But they also encouraged the students' use of informal language or "tech talk," taking "shortcuts and putting less effort into their writing."

Educational software, even that which mimics the long used school workbooks for drill and practice, has advantages over them. They can individualize questions depending on the learner's level of skill, and provide instantaneous feedback which is impersonal. This is an advantage since, from a psychological point of view, error now becomes something to learn from rather than to fear.

Nor does the computer have favorites and so the use of a software program lowers the real and psychological cost of error. This is important because many negative patterns of behavior in school grow out of fear of error and failure. Moreover, word processing on a screen makes correction and revision easier.

If even a small part of teaching basic skills can be accomplished using software, the market for these programs will be huge in the trillion dollar worldwide education market.

Through Children's Minds

Chapter 14

Marketing to Children Which Will Likely Fail

While the presence of children in the marketplace was long recognized, as well as that children might or might not become the future adult customers for a brand, the complexity of marketing to children was not understood. Hearing children sing the line from an adult advertising commercial was considered evidence of sufficient marketing effort. It was believed that the purchasing behavior of children was easily changed through conditioning, much as a "red light halted a runaway horse...galloping down Main Street," this being "a smart animal" the local police chief stated.

This example was used in an old, widely read book by Clyde Miller, *The Power of Persuasion*. Thus, he wrote, "it takes time...but...think of what it can mean to your firm in profits if you can condition a million or ten million children who will grow up into adults trained to buy your product as soldiers are trained to advance when they hear the trigger words, 'forward march.'"

Herb Sheldon, a TV star with a large children's following, commented more than fifty years ago that 'Children are living, talking records of what we tell them every day." Does *any* parent believe this?

Moreover, when dealing with children's health products such as vitamins, marketers must be extremely cautious. While describing a cereal as "tasty" is acceptable, doing the same for a children's vitamin pill would be dangerous and cross the line of what many consider acceptable.

The myth persists that the behavior of children is easily conditioned though conditioning works only with select populations, those having far below average intellectual ability. For them, conditioning so simplifies their environment that they can function better.

Where conditioning is effective, to the degree that it is, this is only in environments where rewards and punishments are tightly controlled such as in prisons. But even with those conditions, conditioning is ineffective in changing the behavior of most prisoners for the recidivism rate is high.

Long ago a social psychologist, Fritz Heider, studied why people credited properties to an object, even to one which exists only in their mind. He concluded that people possess a need to determine what objects are and that they do this by putting together the object's characteristics which they sense.

Similarly, people feel the need to make sense of other people's behavior. To do this they create reasons for their behavior, attributing motives and feelings which will, purportedly, explain it. Heider believed that this activity was ingrained in the human personality. He termed the conclusions which we create about the behavior of others *naive psychology*, or what is ordinarily called "common sense."

For example, if six-year-old Johnny roughly grabbed his four-year-old sister, he may later tell his angry mother that he did so because she was about to fall, hoping that his mother will consider his act to be caring and not, as it was, motivated by anger and jealousy.

The explanations which people give to the behavior of others fall into two categories: internal, that the behavior was caused by a person's ability and attitude; or external, that it was caused by the social situation or environment.

Heider's naive psychology explains many of the mistakes which are made in producing products for

Through Children's Minds

children. That these failed executives followed erroneous notions, based on their personal childhood events, in determining what children should like. *They* had loved "X" and so children *should* love it too. This is like saying that today's youth would prefer a Hula Hoop to an iPad. This type of manager will lose a great deal of money until discovering how unique children really are.

Thus, products whose design relies solely on a manager's personal beliefs are more likely to be bust than blockbuster. An example was Disney's Hunchback figure which might have been OK for a tie-in to adults but was a foreign concept to children.

Most adults cannot think like a child though all were once children. The thought processes which were native to them have since disappeared, and this is fortunate for they would interfere with productive adult activity. Even being a parent does not guarantee accurate knowledge of children.

Thus, children's marketers who do not consider the likes and dislikes of children *must* fail since they do not understand their customer. Then, after producing a product based on faulty knowledge and failing to test-market it, they advertise it with lavish adjectives.

If there is one rule which should be followed in marketing, and particularly with children, it is to be honest. Children are kind and will readily forgive hurtful behavior if they believe that it was unintentional. But they will not easily forgive, or forget, a lie about a product which they were induced to buy or that they asked to be purchased for them. And particularly not a product which causes them to be mocked by their friends!

When I joke with children, I am always the butt of the humor, and the rude comments which are made by the (stuffed) animals in the room are always directed at me.

Through Children's Minds

A seven-year-old girl once asked me why the (stuffed) bear sitting on a chair in the corner of my office called me names. I said that he was the baby in his family and was angry because his older brothers and sisters bossed him around. But because they were bigger, he couldn't say anything to them and so he took his angry feelings out on me. The girl thought for a moment and then said, "It's good that he has a good friend like you," and I agreed.

A *good friend* is what marketer's and store managers must be to their youthful customers. A store wanting young customers must cater to them. As one mother said, "To shop with a two-year-old and a four-year-old is just awful. I'm sure the store is ready to kill me, and it's just very stressful."

Often stores don't relate specifically to children, believing that all customers should be related to identically. The fallacy here is that when a child is not treated well as a potential customer, he will likely *never* become a future customer. Thus, stores should grow customers from their childhood, becoming "kid-friendly" by offering snacks, toys, reading materials, and videos at eye-level, along with promotions by vendors who relate well to children. There can be clubs for children with cumulative rewards for purchases, these developing positive attitudes and allegiance among children.

A parent advisory board can be established through which all proposed children related products and activities would be tested. If parents consider a product to provide little value over existing ones, or that it is fragile, unhealthy, or dangerous, it would be well to scrap the idea. If marketed, the experience can haunt the company by tarnishing its reputation and cause lawsuits.

Parents could be offered samples. Though many parents say that they engage in research before making a

Through Children's Minds

purchase, and particularly a costly one, few actually do so for this requires time and mental and physical effort during which consumption and gratification are delayed.

The value of giving out samples should not be underestimated for some of the most successful American brands were launched in this way. J. B. Stetson initially sent his hat and an order form to merchants in the South West, and Estee Lauder launched her cosmetics empire with free samples.

While the reputation of a company has no importance in the buying decisions of children, the packaging of their product certainly does. Thus it is puzzling why so many companies pay little attention to this factor.

Consider the packaging of milk, a product which is used daily by virtually every American child. While this product is heavily targeted towards children, its packaging could not be more child unfriendly. It is large and clumsy and heavy, difficult to hold and to pour, and the container cannot be easily drunk from. This is not unusual for most packaging is geared towards adults even if the adult spin-offs of products such as candy bars and cereals are intended for children.

But even if the names are made child oriented and the packages become more child attractive with large lettering and bright colors and figures, the marketer's thinking is too often geared toward adults with the different physical and mental states of children being ignored. As if the old-time belief that children were merely small adults still held.

The instructions for many products assume that all purchasers, including children, already know how to open the package and to use the product, And the legal warnings which companies increasingly consider to be essential are unintelligible to virtually all children, they possibly being of greatest use by parents to educate their children in the pronunciation of multi-syllabic words.

Even the understanding of older children cannot be assumed. After my lengthy explanation to a twelve-year-old girl, who had nodded her head in agreement as I spoke, I asked if she understood what I said. "No," she replied.

The packaging of the product is even more important when it is intended for children than for adults. In a self-service store, children are reluctant to approach a salesperson with questions so the package must provide the child with an honest representation of the product, placed at their eye level, using words geared to their level of intellectual and emotional development and physical dexterity. With increasing restrictions on advertising to children, the package's characteristics assume even greater importance.

Perhaps a free, hard plastic carrying case could be provided to children to prevent them from squirting out from the juice-box straw, or children's foods could be sold in re-sealable containers rather than boxes, with single servings for lunch boxes. This would also make sense considering the reduced size of the American family and the far greater number of adults living alone today.

The marketing of even potentially successful children's products may be doomed if their packaging is inadequate since the packaging creates a crucial first impression. And, to paraphrase an old adage, a first impression can be made only once.

The following basic questions should be asked. Is the package easily opened? Is the packaging novel and colorful? Can the instructions be easily read and understood by children?

Marketers who ignore a child's influence on their

Through Children's Minds

parents will also fail. Children are incredibly aware of brands and incredibly brand loyal. The child may not have money in their pocket but in the end they are pretty sure to get what they want from their parents.

Companies with a top management that doesn't fully support marketing to children also court failure. Strategies for new products spring from overall corporate strategy. If a firm has devised new product strategies that relate to children, it should be because top management has decided that children will be an important market for the firm. When viewed as a minor market, children will not receive the same attention that they would at a company which regards them as a significant or total part of their business and inadequate effort will be paid to product development. New products from these companies will likely be brand extensions of adult products rather than developed through long-term innovation.

Another red flag for failure is to lack awareness that each child is somebody's child. Every parent has profoundly strong feelings about their child. The manufacturer and marketer of a product which causes their child unhappiness, and this is definitely true of a product which causes the slightest harm, can expect a major negative response from the child's parents.

Marketing ideas for children's products should not ignore the intrinsic nature of items. As, the unfortunate suggestion by a research company that because stuffed animals are big sellers, a stuffed truck should be produced. Would *any* child cuddle this?

Nor should the Brand Manager System be relied on. The Brand Manager System dates back more than eighty years. It describes the marketing program of a large corporation in which the brand manager has full authority for the development and allocation of advertising efforts. The personal goal of the junior executive, who manages brands with relatively low sales, is to advance swiftly to manage a larger brand with greater sales or a group of brands. Thus the junior manager may seek a short-term sales increase, as with a "hot" advertising concept and a brief, large advertising expenditure.

While the Brand Manager System works with a static market like the archetypical adult housewife, it will not be effective with the children's market which is continually in flux and requires patience and longer-term efforts. When marketing to children, the marketer must think in terms of "this generation" rather than "this year" for though the children's market is divorced from the mainstream of the (adult) consumer market because of its child-like elements, it has increasing adult characteristics.

The children's marketplace is also a market in which the customers are continually new to a brand, this containing the possibility that they will become committed to the brand. To market successfully to children one needs continuous marketing efforts rather than a sporadic promotional burst followed by periods of inactivity. This, because it is a market which changes constantly and is thus a moving time frame.

Chapter 15

Advertising to the Youth Market

The advertising techniques used in both the youth and adult markets are similar, involving a combination of direct and indirect means of communication.

Direct means of communication include print magazines and TV and Internet advertising. Club membership is also used, though mostly with children.

Indirect forms of advertising involve the use of licensed characters and celebrities, and product placement in movies.

A major difference between advertising to adults and advertising to children is that, to retain parental acceptance, it is best that the latter be subtle and contain an educational component.

When Marshall McLuhan wrote "The medium is the message," he meant that each medium has effects on the way people's minds work and are independent of the content being transmitted. Before print, oral language and face-to-face communication were used as the technology of mass communication. It is likely that there are different ways in which people classify, reason, and remember, brought about by different media.

Some research indicates that it is not literacy itself but the interaction between teacher and student which brings about the most widely generalized intellectual skills. This is the same positive effect found for television when parents actively involve children in discussion of what they are viewing. Though watching television and playing video games have been criticized for isolating children, it is important to remember that reading requires solitude for its effective practice.

While there is overlap in the skills needed to gain

Through Children's Minds

information from reading and watching television, the two are relatively independent of each other. A child who is a poor reader may well be able to gain information from a television program, and asking penetrating questions about a television program has been found to increase reading comprehension.

Young children tend to learn what they see on television more thoroughly than what they read, and they gain more information from the visual than the auditory track. This indicates the power of television producers and their need for caution with this audience.

Infants as young as six months have been found to pay attention longer to a television set with a picture on the screen but no sound than to a set emanating sound without a picture. This is logical since children's visual abilities become highly developed during their first year of life, well before they acquire language, and it is their knowledge of the visual world which helps them to decode their mother tongue.

Thus, visual ability is a more basic way of understanding the world than language. Not until the age of seven does adding an audio track to a silent film add anything to children's immediate recall of the film.

Watching television does not reduce the imaginative play of children as some fear though this depends on the program. *Mr. Rogers* and *Sesame Street* were found to stimulate make-believe play, particularly in children who were low in imagination.

If successful, advertisements intended for children can have a broad effect, changing not only their attitudes and behavior but that of their parents and peers, encouraging their favorable attitudes towards the product and increasing the likelihood of its purchase.

There are three goals which all advertising towards children have: to cause the child to make a purchase or to

Through Children's Minds

visit a store; to have the child persuade their parents to do so; to have the child favor the product and, more importantly, the brand when they become adult.

For advertising to effect behavior and attitudes is no simple matter and particularly when it involves children for advertising to them is governed by stringent regulations. Advertisements for children are forbidden to: imply that not having a product will make a child inferior to their peers; frighten a child or encourage violent or antisocial behavior; employ props which are not available with the product as it is sold; place breakfast food outside the context of a balanced diet, and others.

These can be summarized in one assertion, with which no one can disagree: Be honest! Or as has been joked, "Honesty is the best policy. I've tried everything else."

Yet while some commercials may be viewed as misleading and manipulative, there is no set norm for what constitutes an unacceptable level of deception. The suggestion has been made that there be an interdisciplinary panel of judges composed of parents, marketers, psychologists, and others, to pre-examine advertisements for deception.

It has also been suggested that the Federal Trade Commission assume a more active role by developing educational advertisements to teach children consumer skills, that elementary school systems teach children the purpose of advertising and how to interpret the selling intent of the message, and that families be encouraged to take an active role in explaining to children the purpose of advertising and how to evaluate a commercial.

Yet being honest when advertising to children is not a simple matter since their communication skills are not fully formed and the essence of advertising is to gain the attention of the audience and to effectively communicate with them.

Just as marketers who create children's products based solely on their childhood preferences must fail, so will copywriters who believe that because they understand their own children, they understand all children. A parent's knowledge of their children is partial and gaining even this requires years of interaction between the parent and their child during which the parent learns to interpret their child's subtle verbal and behavioral clues, a goal which they never completely achieve.

How often does every parent ask their child, "How could you *do* that?" Considering this common experience, how knowledgeable can one be of children who experience other families and possibly other cultures too?

The marketer must be particularly careful when advertising food products to children for they have been found to believe many of the product claims made about advertised foods including aspects as varied as a product's size, its ability to make you smile, and general health claims.

Research showed that children who were exposed to a comparative nutritional claim about the relative number of vitamins in one candy bar as opposed to another were more likely to perceive the product as having lots of vitamins as contrasted with children who were presented the same vitamin information about the product without a comparison. Other research revealed that most children do not have any clear sense of what a "balanced breakfast" is, being unable to specify its content.

Studies have shown that children would prefer to eat a cereal in which a liked animated figure (one that gets their own way, has fun, has a curious appearance)

Through Children's Minds

was present and liked the cereal (an inferred endorsement). Younger children and children from less affluent families even believed that these characters knew which cereals children should eat.

Children's requests to their parents and their consumption of advertised foods and frequency of eating at fast food restaurants has been found to correlate with the amount of their Saturday morning television viewing.

Communicating with a child is not easy. Even when they are older the speech of youth can be easily misinterpreted. Today, the term "dating" has a vastly different meaning than during my youth.

Young children must learn to interpret the information and cues which advertisements present. Otherwise, the ad is but a jumble of action and words, easily forgotten though creating anxiety for parents and activity by government regulators.

Studies have shown that even children between the age of three and six can distinguish the commercial from the program, and between programs which they or their parents would like, including older and younger children too. Yet it can seem otherwise because of the language limitations of children in this age range and their shyness in relating to adults who are strangers.

Psychologists have long known that what a young child is willing or able to verbalize is not a true indicator of what the child understands. There is a distinction between the *active* vocabulary and the *understanding* vocabulary.

The active vocabulary is what is expressed and relates to the notion of language "performance" as opposed to language "competence." The understanding vocabulary refers to the greater number and variety of words that are understood than are spoken.

While painful to accept ignorance, when writing

advertisements for children adopting a humble attitude is often best. Recognizing adult limitations, it has been suggested that children create advertisements for children though I would trust this as much as I would having children interview other children to learn about their worries. So though it requires both time and money, conducting research is essential when creating new children's products and advertisements intended for children.

What is clear or familiar to adults, may not be to children or teenagers and age is not a reliable guide to understanding. Much of what is readily understood by virtually all adults would not be understood by many children, and this ability can differ even amongst children of the same age.

And, just as with adults, what captures children's interest will differ. The eyes of a four-year-old will become transfixed by the play of another child who bounces a ball tethered to a paddle, a sight which older children and teenagers and adults ignore.

The complexity of advertising to children can perhaps be best appreciated by recognizing the intricacy of play though it is an activity which is engaged in by all children and adults regardless of their family background, social class, or culture.

Though play is important in human development it is easier to observe than to define. This is because there is no single set of behaviors which define it. An infant explores objects by manipulating them, a toddler exhibits sensorimotor practice, and older children and adults create art or stories. One can play with others or alone, with games possessing rules, or those which are imaginary.

Yet despite the difficulty with its definition, play contains common characteristics. Its motivation is an internal demand rather than an external one. The play itself, rather than its outcome, is what is important, and the player is actively involved.

Play grants individual meaning to objects. Non-rule based, pretend play is inherently free and individual. Finally, play involves joy, this being the *intrinsic motivation* which fosters both play and learning and derives from fully using one's abilities.

Play is particularly important with children for it enables them to learn about their world and to express this knowledge. Play indicates their language, motor skills, social and emotional development, and information about such traits as their persistence and interests. The wide ranging arena encompassed by play has long included early childhood education, and psychotherapy too, that which is geared toward the youngest children being termed *play therapy*.

All communication, which include advertisements, must first be deciphered to have impact. Even the meaning of the simple red traffic signal must be learned. Now consider the complexity of the following toy ad. A pre-teen shoots at his friend with a toy rifle loaded with foam pellets. Gripped by excitement and fantasy, the child, after viewing the commercial, ignores its warnings that the proper safety equipment must be worn and that the play should be conducted only under adult supervision. You can imagine the potential outcome.

Yet even with such benign products as snacks, miscommunication can be rife. The meaning of "healthy" when referring to a snack bar is understood by adults to mean that it does not contain excessive fat or sugar or calories and is suitable for an occasional treat. But to a child, "healthy" may be interpreted as indicating that no other food is required, that they can survive in good health on only this food.

Through Children's Minds

Research is needed to reveal whether the accurate meaning of an advertisement is gained by its intended audience. Perhaps the phrase "is healthy" need be expanded to "is healthy when eaten along with other good foods."

Because play is very much on a young child's mind, inattention can easily occur though this experience is common with adults too. Consider an adult's state of mind before a serious date.

The difficulties which those who construct advertisements for children confront fall into four categories: that the language capacities of children can vary greatly, and not only by age; that emotion-laden events such as death, which triggers sadness for adults, may be experienced differently by children; that non-verbal communication, as that which is comprised of sounds and colors, must be learned; and that adult values must be learned, as that a twenty-dollar bill laying on a road is of greater interest than the squirrel who hops by it.

Moreover, unlike adults who prefer white spaces and clean lines and blocks of text, children like clutter: pictures and words and puzzles and odd facts and short text which take up every inch of a page.

And unlike with adults, age counts. My favorite riddle is the following question: What do bears like to do when they go to Niagara Falls? The correct answer, which is that they go over it in *bearrels*, is considered hilarious by younger children but earns an appalled look from older ones.

Children's great natural curiosity makes them receptive to advertisements for ads can teach them something new. Advertising errors can be avoided by seeking the advice of professionals who understand children, and by gaining the opinion of parents having

Through Children's Minds

children of the age which the commercials target. The use of a focus group, to seek the opinions of children themselves, would also be helpful. For this, and to assure objectivity, using a company unrelated to the creator of the advertisement would be best.

These activities are worth the additional time and cost to be sure of the advertisement's effectiveness and public acceptability.

Through Children's Minds

Chapter 16

How Children Relate to Television

Watching television is pervasive in a child's life. The reason for this is easily understandable for the television screen conveys a happy mood anytime it is turned on.

Children begin watching television at an early age, by the age of two, this exposure gradually increasing until the age of six when more than ninety percent of all children view some television daily. A child's involvement with television is far greater than with any other media, most children having considerable experience with television before they see their first movie.

It has been estimated that by the time that children graduate from high school, they have viewed three-hundred-fifty-thousand televised commercial messages. But the phrase, "television viewing of children," is imprecise. As with adults, it can range from paying rapt attention to merely being in a room in which a television is playing.

To paraphrase George Elliot, children live from hand-to-mouth, having a small family of immediate desires. Marketers try to gain a competitive niche for their product in that "small family of immediate desires."

The popular hypothesis that children imitate what they view on television has never been proven. It derives from the simplistic belief that television programs are complex and that children's viewing modes are simple whereas children's viewing styles are, at the very least, more intricate.

The learning that takes place when children view television is more generalized than occurs in school.

Through Children's Minds

Children sense the hidden message in television programs is that they are to be amused. Therefore they mentally simplify the complex stimuli in a program so that they can make sense of it. Thus when children view television they unconsciously seek material which demands minimal attention and little reliance on memory to avoid stressing their inner resources.

Underlying a child's individual response to an individual program or to images within a program is the general condition of television viewing which they have learned. Children do not have high expectations for what television offers. They do not associate it with the kind of pleasure that comes from reading or with the level of demand made in school.

Children bring to television a readiness to be pleased which contrasts strongly with their capacity to learn. Thus they do not notice the signs of class and racism which critics like to explore. Because of their inattention, children are not susceptible to what some like to consider the "mass audience effect" in which attitudes are blindly adopted.

The perfect stimulus is one which does not make demands by being either too loud or too soft, and is neither too little nor too much. It is a perfect balance of elements. Television, through its combination of sound and picture and its overall tone, achieves this balance. It does not impose too much on children nor does it demand too much involvement from them. It can be turned on and related to with little effort.

Thus when children watch television they expect to be entertained through easily recognized, clearly presented images, and the pervading tone. They remember programs which they have seen but not its details. Yet when placed in the right conditions, they can recall many visual details in a show but do not often do

Through Children's Minds

so. They do not consider this task significant, or expect to be asked for these details.

The mind is not always thinking of the events surrounding it. Children recall little of what they have seen on television because they are not applying the part of their mind that they use to describe or to analyze what they see. They view television with indifference, and resent any demand that they should derive significant meanings from it.

Just as during other periods of semi-boredom, when watching television, children let their minds wander, on a level beneath that of language whose function is to describe experience.

During the course of their development, children learn images earlier than they learn words. This "primitive" capacity exists and is used during television viewing in which one image is focused upon while the background sounds and images remain. Familiar images and their associations induce a mood that incorporates the differences between programs. Content and context, with its mixture of auditory and visual clues and familiar remarks, are so entwined that children find them almost impossible to distinguish and to determine which elements are important and which are incidental. This is why there is uniformity in their tastes, expectations, and level of recall.

Children gradually become familiar with images they perceive as being fixed like the face of the hero, or become a ritual series of actions like the car chase. They become familiar with the context in which these images or actions occur, whether a thriller or a situation comedy.

Television viewing, the viewing of complex pictures, arouses the capacity to deal with multiple pieces of information simultaneously through parallel processing whereas reading, during which a person processes one piece of information at a time, utilizes serial processing. And just as one must learn a code in order to be able to read, there is also a code which must be learned in order to view television and movies successfully

Watching television is a skill which children gradually develop. Young children sometimes believe that by changing channels they can see different parts of the same character's body; or that when a character is off-screen they still exist, alive and well, in the video.

While gaining television literacy, children must learn that when two images occur in progressively shorter, quicker fragments, they are converging on each other dramatically or spatially, and that when a camera zooms in on a detail it communicates a relationship between that detail and its larger context.

They must learn that a faceless narrator implies that they are distant from the scene; and that a visual signal such as a fade serves as punctuation.

Boys and girls don't differ much in the amount of television they watch and have some favorite shows in common. But gender differences show up early and grow larger as children age.

Very young children, those under three or so, consider all television except cartoons to be real. Later, for a few more years, they believe that what they see on television *probably* happens in the real world, and particularly if the person on the screen is like someone they know.

Before children attend school they prefer programs with animals, animated characters, and puppets in a story format with much laughter and slapstick action. Older children (approximately six to seven) prefer child oriented adventure and variety programs, cartoons, and game shows. A visual trick will

Through Children's Minds

make far more impact than the outline of a plot.

Children of eight to ten years also prefer these programs though movies become increasingly important. By the time a child leaves elementary school, their viewing interests are more similar to adults than pre-school children.

As is apparent in the long success of *Sesame Street* in teaching children to read, this program borrowed many techniques from TV commercials: using short messages, and realistically executed fantasy; using repetition; emphasizing motion rather than talking; and showing how enjoyment results from success.

Children recognize books as fictional earlier than television since print does not look like what it symbolizes. Producers must continually remind themselves of how inadequate the cognitive capacities of children are, and that this makes younger viewers more susceptible to messages from television than older ones.

By speaking with their child, parents can play an important role in helping the child to separate the television world from the real world, changing them from passive viewers into active critics.

A very young child may view a movie character who has the capacity to turn into a monster as two separate characters. The ability to follow subplots, or to sense eeriness or danger through subtle visual and auditory cues, is absent in children though some gain elements of it early. I was recently surprised when a five-year-old boy quickly grasped the subtly expressed lack of romantic interest of a babysitter in her younger charge in an episode on the Disney Channel show, *JESSIE*. Still, the capacity to grasp complex plots and scenes and recurrent plot formats, as by anticipating what is going to happen next, isn't fully formed in most children until adolescence.

Through Children's Minds

Thus when producing a program for young children, the understanding of these basic visual techniques should not be assumed for their grasping of these techniques affect how well the production will be understood.

These early childhood limitations impress the importance of care in childhood productions lest its very young viewers try for themselves the dangerous activities which their TV "friends" perform so successfully.

Television programs must be produced which fit the child. A direct reproduction of real-life activity, as by merely viewing a pre-school on the screen, will fail to interest their intended audience. The weaknesses of television as a medium lies in the passivity of the viewer and their inability to use their imagination.

But television can be valuable for educational or social purposes. Research has shown that having characters of minority groups (racial, ethnic, disabled), increased the children's interest in these groups and raised self-confidence.

The effect of viewing even one such show on children should not be discounted. Many years before the advent of television it was found that viewing *The Birth of a Nation,* a classic movie which presented the Ku Klux Klan in a positive light and the freed American slaves negatively, caused a significant, persisting negative increase in the attitude of white pre-adolescents and adolescents toward African-Americans, the effect of this attitude shift being cumulative and depending on the number of films with the same theme being viewed.

The fact that unpredictability adds interest to a production explains why producing programs for adolescents and adults can be more difficult than for young children: it is not easy for the program's creator to remain many steps ahead of their adult audience so that

Through Children's Minds

they can't predict the plot.

Children find action and sound effects more attractive than dialogue because visual movement attracts their attention and makes information easier to remember. Young children remember information better from a narrated television story than they do from the same story read to them from a picture book, the explicit TV story being easier to understand than the implicit actions in the story book.

Programs which are the easiest for children to follow have a recurring song and the repeated behavior of familiar characters. From this familiarity the child can built into the more complex elements of the show.

Children look for expected clues but do not easily discriminate between that which is significant and that which isn't. All programs have some details that will attract their attention and many details that do not. An odd clue might fit in with other of their mental associations, and this is why there can seem to be little logic to the statements they make about their viewing activity.

Television is entertainment and the purpose of its images is to provide a familiar context for the next appearance of the same program and not anything beyond the confines of the television experience. Children mentally ignore much of what they see and concentrate on the familiar. Adults relate similarly to television but are better at disguising this through explanation when they are asked.

Children relate to television's blend of word and image because it is easier than concentrating on one or the other. This causes their less sharp attention to what is on the screen while they gain the basic pleasure of television with its mixture of movement and imagery and colors. These are more important than the information

Through Children's Minds

being communicated.

While children can recall what they see, they tend not to, and children over the age or seven or eight relate to television with the same sophisticated sense as do adults. They expect television to provide undemanding entertainment, which is also unimportant. This is why the more that television is watched, the less closely it is watched, and there is an increased inability to recall what has been seen.

Viewers do not become silent, passive zombies, or describable in any similarly colorful phrase. But television is unimportant, though many children say that they would be bored if there were not television to watch or video games to play.

While children can respond with interest, television encourages inattentiveness and indifference to information. Thus children merely discriminate between what interests them or not.

The most effective commercial on television is its advertisement for itself: entertainment lacking demand, and easily forgotten as part of a daily routine.

Children select images to make sense of what they see, grasping its structure and remembering individual points. They relate to television as they do to the street scene while strolling with their parents, passing by much and forgetting most, remembering only a little if it is striking enough or if there is a personal association that makes it interesting.

Repeated items or images become remembered, Advertisements, which children consider thirty second entertainment, provide most of what they recall, not in terms of elements of the product but in the jingles or catch-phrases that are associated with them.

When children remember part of a televised series it is not always the most recent episode. A scene can leave

Through Children's Minds

a deeper impression, a moment that frightened them or is associated with some personal experience.

The image of the highly recalled hero works against having more than a minimal memory of the plot. There is an overall image of the series with one program merging with another, and images within a program being incorporated within the larger image of the entire program.

Series have typical gestures which dominate over individual plots. Thus the recurring situation is usually remembered but not the most recent episode.

Children look for and remember what they choose to see and with thrillers, actions are more important than plot. Thus when the hero chases the bad guy in their predictable routine, children recognize the expected and enjoy it. Children see the violence depicted in a series as being part of the style of the program which removing it would destroy. Verbal aggression and ridicule create more upset in children than physical aggression since those can be more easily related to their own lives.

Because the mind can only process a certain amount of information at a time, it seeks clues for what is significant and ignores the rest.

Children "see" and remember more than they can report, with familiar material being stored and accumulating in their memory. But there are limits on what can be stored subconsciously so, when questioned, children recount one or two of the program's central images, having concentrated on those details that make a program recognizable.

There is a ritual to television programs with the viewer expecting a central imagery and a balance between repetition of the familiar and the unexpected. Children look forward to the familiar and this is why the formulaic actions of the hero are so much better remembered than is the plot. Familiarity breeds remembrance.

The power of television to convey information is limited without an external aid, such as parent involvement. Complex visual images do not automatically create learning. Even *Sesame Street* was later found to have limited educational value unless mothers played a role with their additional enthusiasm. This is contrary to the findings from early research with specially selected children.

Learning is complex and expectations influence the way in which children approach the information offered to them as do their individual personalities. Children do not associate television with learning but with play though they can parrot ads with educational justifications for purchases which they want their parents to make.

Children choose what kind of information to take in and what to regard as unneeded. For many children, the inessential means anything that is not entertaining. Children will watch anything which entertains them and the attempts to make educational programs more entertaining by including humor made a difference in the amount that children were prepared to watch but little difference in their ability to learn.

Children will not learn from television unless they grant other than their usual way of relating to it. There is no relationship between visual attention and the ability to remember though educational programs are designed around this assumption.

Children recall better when the central point of the program is presented through special effects and action than when it is presented mostly verbally. They remember gestures and characteristics of humor and facial expression and the opening sequence or the

Through Children's Minds

familiar tune of programs but don't analyze it or base their behavior upon it. Through repetition, children learn more of emotional atmosphere and gestures and attitude than hard facts or stereotypes of the world. Thus much of what they remember is vague and trivial.

Contrary to the fear that television will change social attitudes for the worse, as radio did for Germany with the rise of Nazism, what television does is far more to reinforce those opinions which are already held than to change them. The ability to shut out opinions is as strong as the ability to retain information.

Unlike in school where children must please the teacher, television makes no such demand. The picture is always moving and someone is always talking without seeking their attention, leaving them undisturbed. Great, potentially anxiety arousing issues are subconsciously rejected; the small, unimportant ones are absorbed.

For this reason, children pay less attention to and tend to dislike news and documentaries for these make demands on them and are less familiar. In one study, in which children were shown the identical lecture both live and on television, they enjoyed the live lecture but resented the televised lecture. Children consider as "boring" those televised programs which they sense are making demands on them for television is associated in their minds with an absence of challenge.

Children often combine watching television with other activities, playing with toys or eating, their attention to the screen not being high even at the most intense moments. They bring their own attitudes to television, attending to the recognizable clues and gaining the minimum amount of information needed without difficulty.

Children assume that television does not demand nor deserve concentration or strenuous involvement, the

Through Children's Minds

act of watching being more important than the content. This is why children tend to be loyal to their favorite programs, having formed a habit in viewing the familiar and expected. When asked to remember what they viewed on television, children tend to be baffled. This seems an odd question for, unlike with school, they do not approach television with the attitude of learning something but to relax.

To attempt to fit types of children to different tastes in programs is to ignore their pre-set expectations of all programs and the variety of different attitudes within one program. Children pay great attention to the least demanding program and ignore those which make great demand on them. Most of the time, children watch all shows without concern for what is going on, reacting or not to what they view. But they are nearly always aware of the differences between popular characters and the importance of the roles they play.

For the child, the personality is the program, with their actions, stunts, and recognizable characteristics maintaining it. Children remember a series in terms of the repeated actions of the heroes; television heroes are important for what they *do* and not who they are. Children have no particular interest in the sex of the hero with many series being popular with both boys and girls.

A series' success lies in sustaining automatic associations and fulfilling expectations from one week to the next. That the character wears a particular hat or repeats the same phrase or that two central characters have a type of interaction is more important than that he/she shoots people, for the former characteristic(s) renders them a distinctive personality.

Children are as aware of the underlying ritual of the program as they are of the names of the actors, with each episode of the series confirming this recognition.

Through Children's Minds

The gimmicks vary but the recognition factors remain constant and, against this, the variations from one episode to another are minor.

This ease of recognition is the glue which holds the series together and is why a series can retain its popularity, and provide a ready market, for years after it goes off the air.

When children see people killed or noses being broken they view these scenes without any sense of moral stricture or deep emotional involvement. They recognize them merely as things which the character does. It is this which appeals to them rather than the plot of the episode or the mystery which is being solved. Thus, the star of the show becomes stereotyped and this attracts children to the show. The gimmicks vary but the recognition characteristics of the star remain constant.

For children, that a woman is a cleaning woman does not reflect on the role of women in society. What is important is that this character becomes a jaw-breaking, crime fighter, it being the character's transformation into a powerful figure which they note. This attracts them because it is the power which they would like to possess in their world, one which is controlled by powerful adults: their parents and teachers and others.

Television series which lack repeated recognition factors and intriguing gimmicks are unlikely to find favor with children. And contrary to parents' worries, children are perfectly aware of their limited capacities in the real world and do not identify with the characters they favor or try to imitate their behavior.

Children do not become amoral but have learned the rituals of action thrillers: that the leading figure exhibits the most power and survives at the end of the episode. Which *must* happen if they are to appear on screen the following week.

Through Children's Minds

What children want is to become powerful and beautiful and rich and famous and on TV when they are older. What they learn from their favored personalities are the advantages of fame and money.

Younger children like their hero's ability to do stunts, to drive fast or win every race, but they are aware of the fantasy involved and do not take the stunts seriously. Older children see these characters realistically, as actors who are paid a lot of money. They collect information about them but do not identify with them and the more they learn about them the more they identify them as actors.

The most disliked characters are those who talk rather than act, and those who draw too much attention to themselves, "a show off." The more personality intrudes over the action, the easier it is for children to dismiss the character as being boring or stupid. Heroes have distinctive roles to play, experiencing suffering but coming out happy in the end.

Though children like horror films and thrillers they do not enjoy being scared. The presence of many shootings on a TV show can be less frightening than one shooting, for the former is an integral part of a recognized ritual whereas the one killing can be emotionally compelling and remembered long after the show. Thus, parents would do well to take seriously a news program's caution that an imminent film clip may not be suitable viewing for children. But a scene from a fictional show which mirrored an incident in a child's life can be equally upsetting.

Television is not a conveyor of fantasy that is taken seriously as if it were real and carried moral weight. Children have a complex relationship between the fantastic and the real, being able to distinguish between dangers in real life and invented fantasies on the screen.

Through Children's Minds

Violence is not perceived as such for children know that the murders and car chases are part of the ritual of drama in which the hero wins out in the end. They know the real names and favorite clothes and colors and other likes and dislikes of the stars and are aware of those who act and those who are personalities in their own right.

Of stars which they prefer, girls tend to go for their looks and kindness; boys are more impressed by their strength, though being funny, making them laugh, is equally important. Only as children become older teenagers do they begin to appreciate the quality of the acting.

Children's statements about television reflect pleasure but also boredom for they associate television watching with having nothing better to do and a way of reducing boredom. Inattentive viewing which lacks emotion is the norm.

Though what children like most is to watch familiar programs, they can also gain information from what they see. If a child loves animals, they will tend to watch a nature show and to learn from it. Children are capable of paying attention to programs as strongly as television producers like to think always takes place though, in general, children expect to see nothing memorable on the screen, having gained the expertise of watching television

Children have difficulty distinguishing between the significant and the insignificant and television provides a complex mixture of picture and music and talk to interpret as compared to books. They must learn what is real and what is make-believe, what is "live" and what is rehearsed. While children are attracted to the most visually active and novel parts of television programs, there is no correlation between this and what they remember. In other words, the more stimulation

Through Children's Minds

presented, the less is learned.

When children find something interesting, they pay attention. But their attention level soon lowers for they know that the program material will soon change and become less interesting.

The moving television pictures create the *marginal awareness* experienced by both children and adults when they glance over information rather than study it. This is why, when reading a book during which more and a different type of attention is demanded, children are more horrified by a violent scene than when the same scene is viewed on television for television is considered to present entertainment and be unworthy of serious attention. Yet this is not so different from how adults view television for research has shown that adults watch the screen only three-quarters of the time, even during an exciting movie.

Television offers children the undemanding pleasure which they want and children respond to this offer, viewing the screen for hours a day. They know the shows they like, cartoons before the age of six and, later, increasingly adult programs like thrillers and situation comedies. Children dislike news programs because they are too serious and too verbal, though they will relate to personal news: a local murder or weather crisis or accident but not to a war which killed thousands of people far away. So even if children are watching the news with their family, it goes unseen unless the item is local and thus distinguishable from their generalized reaction of "watching television."

Children do not watch only their favorite programs. Their loyalty to a program is reduced by their need to watch television for its own sake and children often view simply what is on at the time they want. "Late night" shows are considered anything after 7:30PM by

Through Children's Minds

seven and eight-year-olds. Thus, most children view some adult programs which many parents would consider unsuitable for children. Despite this, studies have found that most parents do not permit their children to see anything they want to watch.

When they were asked, children knew what their parents did not want them to watch (as, thrillers) but did not feel prevented in doing so. And even if they did, they managed to see these shows.

Parents tend to give conventional "correct" answers to questions, as do children. Parents state that they would prevent children from watching certain programs and children state that they would prevent their younger siblings or friends from watching certain programs, violent shows with murder and blood, those which are their favorites. Both children and parents tend to say what they feel they should though behaving differently.

While television has long been criticized as being a wasteland, it is also a great educator for the television screen holds images of life styles and nations that most people can only dream of experiencing and visiting.

To create a truly educational program is not easy though many try, calling a program "educational" though no producer considers it that. The president of a children's TV network stated the problem clearly: "I've seen a lot of ideas that were very earnest and educational but no child in the world would want to watch them. The single biggest problem is figuring out innovative ways to blend in entertainment. We don't have a captive audience the way a teacher does,"

While playing Chutes and Ladders with a four-year-old girl, this board game rewarding good behavior and punishing bad behavior, she suddenly said, apropos of nothing outside of her, "Don't do drugs. They're not good." I later learned from her mother that the statement derived from a TV show which she had recently watched.

Television serves to lower the advantage possessed by middle-class people in the world of schools and books, and can aid educational development in the Third World. Though it cannot close the knowledge gap created by society, studies of *Sesame Street* in the United States and Australia and Israel have shown that disadvantaged groups did learn what was taught on the show, and that they learned more if they watched more.

The Children's Television Workshop show, *The Electric Company*, an experiment in using television to teach reading skills to second through fourth-grade children who were having difficulty learning to read, attracted a large audience and was highly successful. All groups, black and white and Spanish-speaking and English-speaking, benefitted equally from the program. Watching television was second nature to these children unlike (unfortunately) reading books.

The program's setting was an urban scene and music and humor were used to concretely present difficult reading concepts that a teacher using print can present only abstractly. Making letters bright and expanding them at the moment when they were being pronounced added clarity to the task being learned, and "blending" this with the sight of the moving lips brought attention to the mouth, these being helpful in learning to read.

But what is crucial to learning via television is the presence of an adult to encourage the child to pay attention, and to make interpretations and explain what the child does not understand. In schools, the teacher is the adult who is present; parents can play this role at home.

Despite the anxiety of some in the media industry,

Through Children's Minds

children aren't from another planet and their way of viewing programs is more similar to an adult's than it seems. So if a child changes the channel it's not because they have a short attention span but because they don't find the program enjoyable.

Through Children's Minds

Chapter 17

What Makes Children's Television Commercials Effective?

All who view television commercials, including children, usually don't credit opinions which conflict with their own. They are suspicious of such content. Only with minor matters, such as the preference for one brand over another, can television change opinions. The more vague and emotional the appeal of the commercial, the greater is the chance of having an impact.

The basic principle which underlies all advertising is to combine product recognition with an existing pattern of behavior or an attitude. This is most likely to happen by telling a wonderful story which the viewer wants to believe.

Being persuasive is difficult since the more obvious is the desire to persuade, the less likely will be the success. A remark that one overhears casually is more persuasive than a long, logical argument. It is for this reason that only a small proportion of the advertisements on television give information about the product that is being sold.

When too much attention is drawn to the presentation for a product, the audience will react against it. This is why the major goal of advertisers is first to entertain with providing facts being second. They are afraid that their audience, not liking argument and recognizing that their minds are being challenged, will react with *defensive avoidance* against the product.

While repetition is important, the key to success is to repeat enough to persuade the potential customer but not so much that you annoy them. Being overly insistent

Through Children's Minds

is least successful when trying to persuade someone.

Similarly, just as children dislike personalities who attract too much attention to themselves, they show the least interest in advertisements which insist on their message or compare itself to similar brands. Ads with high-pressure sales talk are criticized by children for their lack of humor. The more forceful are the claims, the more suspicious are children, feeling that they are being "got at."

Unfortunately, advertisers sometimes write for each other and their corporate clients rather than for their audience. They ignore the basic rule of advertising that changing a habit of purchase is more easily done by manipulating an existing motive than generating a new one.

Nearly all children like most televised ads. They see them as entertaining programs and the better for being repeated. They are shorts that are funny or contain interesting characters or an odd incident. The product advertised is not as important as the style of the presentation and the characters.

The main reasons which children give for liking advertisements are the personalities, the gimmicks, the humor, and the songs. Of these techniques, humor is the most appreciated and advertisements that rely on a serious message create a negative reaction against the message. Humor is a way of not pushing a message too far, of avoiding the boomerang effect and defensive avoidance that occurs if a message is stressed too continuously.

Advertisers believe that children are most influenced by advertisements for products that appeal to them, as snacks and candy, and that these have an effect on buying habits and recall. But children's favorite advertisements are often not for products that are

Through Children's Minds

intended to appeal to them or even of interest to them, like banks and cleaning sprays.

Children remember the advertisement's gimmick far more readily than the brand name with which it is associated. And although children are used to influence their parents, children can distinguish between advertisements as entertainment and their attempt to influence buying habits.

Children's sophistication about advertisements increases as they grow older. They might be influenced to buy certain products but they know that they are being coaxed to do so. The implied claim, that eating a snack will give one great powers or some such thing, is not important to them. One research study found that nutrition and health themes for a snack bar appealed to children as well as the more traditional richness and sweetness themes.

Children gain the capacity to distinguish which toys are intended for them from the gender implied in the commercials. The toys for boys contain more toy action, frequent cuts, sound effects, and loud music while the toys which are intended for girls are "softer" in tone and contain more dissolves and background music.

As children grow older they are better able to distinguish between the product and its presentation. Children under the age of seven have a greater tendency to believe their favorite advertisement but by the age of twelve only about ten percent of children believe what their favorite advertisement says.

Thus, the response of children to commercials is complex. They enjoy the advertisement as fantasy but don't believe its commercial appeal. The only thing that they do believe is that the product is available in the store. The notion of "truth" doesn't enter into the equation since the products are being presented as part of a fantasy

Through Children's Minds

world in which snacks and candy and monkeys talk.

There is an off-hand assertive tone to the language of advertisers. Softly, with a friendly, knowing attitude, they encourage the viewer to "try" a product, doing this with the same lack of seriousness which pervades television programming. Advertisers try to create a commercial which is as effective as a casual, throwaway remark, one which is easy to listen to and spoken with conviction.

Children tend to remember advertisements for the same reason that they do their favorite programs. Both repeat clichés and images and, just like successful politicians, their comments are brief and simple.

Entertaining ads, including those which are intended for adults, are remembered, as are brand names. Children look forward to advertisements just as they do to their favorite programs though the scheduling of advertisements is unknown.

Children recall advertisements and their catchy phrase more than other programs because of their repetition. The brand name becomes like the title of a program. It is easy to listen to and to repeat and children gain pleasure from these jingles with the songs and catch phrases having an almost magical allure.

The remembrance of brand names is powerful. I still remember Ipana toothpaste from my childhood though this brand disappeared from American shelves decades ago; and I recognized another ancient brand, Brylcreem men's hair dressing, in my novel (*Ghosts and Angels*), and its advertising jingle too ("A Little Dabb'll Do Ya").

Unlike adults, children under the age of nine are more likely to say that they have been influenced by advertisements. As they get older they tend, like adults, to deny this. In research, those children who said that

Through Children's Minds

they had been influenced cited mostly toys and especially those which were shown near Christmas. They said that they looked forward to advertisements to know what to ask for.

Advertisements offer a miniature version of what children like best about television: slight information with many songs, much humor, and stunts. What they enjoy are the visual techniques, the cartoon characters, and the sense of watching a short, interesting, familiar, repeated program that it would not be fatal to miss. Commercials containing these features maintain children's interest whatever their product.

Though children like advertisements for their own sake and are aware of products being advertised, the information which they gain about products is vague, akin to stating that they like a game because "I like games" or "It is nice." Children who object to advertisements do so because it interrupts their favorite programs.

Children relate to television commercials as follows. A child brings to the screen their unique background, experience, needs, personality, and ability to process information.

Consider a child who is watching television when a commercial for a snack food appears. Lack of interest or momentary inattention may cause the child to not respond to the commercial. If the child does become aware of the commercial, they may selectively attend to the message in a way similar to an adult. Their understanding of the advertisement's content depends on their ability to reason which is influenced by their family experiences and psychological makeup, and is affected by the program's content, the time of day, and with whom they are watching television.

The child may not respond to the commercial. If

they do respond to it, their response may be directed toward the product or toward the commercial or toward both. The response could be an emotional one, such as anger that their mother won't allow them snack foods, or affective, such that the commercial was fun, or evaluative, as, "I like that kind of food."

A motor response may then occur in which the child walks toward the kitchen to find a similar snack, which they enjoy. This response may be remembered by the child and will later affect their willingness to view the commercial again, their feelings about the product, and their intention to purchase or to request purchase of the product. They may even pull their parent away from another activity to see the commercial.

After the purchase is made, the child may create awareness of the product amongst their friends by showing them the product. The child's satisfaction or dissatisfaction with the product may be remembered and affect: his responsiveness to commercials; his feelings toward that particular brand of snack food or snack foods in general; what he tells his friends, and possibly whether they or his parents will buy the product again.

Children proclaim strong opinions though it would be just as sensible for them to hold a different point of view. They exaggerate their enthusiasm for liking or knowing something based on a scrap of fact which contains more than a shadowing of gray.

Estimates of how many children view television are imprecise and may be off by as much as twenty percent depending on how the measure is gained, whether from a child's general estimate, their unsupervised diary, a measurement by older siblings or the child's parent, or an interview of the child. Most studies are done with small samples over brief periods and are difficult to generalize from.

Through Children's Minds

While many people believe that Saturday morning is the most popular time for children's television viewing, it represents fewer hours than prime time, between 8PM and 9PM, when programs have huge children and teen audiences. Prime time shows reach children and parents watching programs together, this reinforcing the connection between a child's desire and their purchasing influence over their parents.

But some nonprime-time programs have a high concentration of young viewers in specific age groups indicating their appeal to that target.

The younger the child, the more likely they are to continue the attention which they paid to the program during the commercial, Older children (9-12 years) tend to talk more during commercials, and the paying of full attention to commercials during prime time viewing decreases with age. Regardless of the length of the commercial, older children pay less attention to commercials than do younger children.

In a study of children between the age of six and twelve, 5-6 years olds were very vulnerable to misleading television advertising; and 7-10 year olds could describe fair principles of advertising but admitted that they could not really evaluate advertising. Their responses to advertising claims depended largely on they having had personal experiences with misleading advertising. Only 11-12 year olds could carefully evaluate the content of television advertising.

Another study found that most advertising disclaimers are inadequately worded, and do not increase children's understanding of the expected performance of a product.

While children generally believe in commercials they like and like commercials which they believe, there is no relationship between a child's impression of the

Through Children's Minds

truthfulness of a commercial and their reasons for liking or disliking it. Recall also does not differ significantly for liked or disliked commercials.

Younger children and those viewing the most commercials have the greatest liking for commercials, and because they like the product being advertised.

Children trust commercials less as they see more of them and as they grow older, from 65% at the first grade level to just 7% by the fifth grade, this decline in trust being based on children's increasing understanding that the purpose of commercials is to persuade.

Commercial research firms tend to find higher levels of persuasion than do studies conducted by consumer advocates. Measures of this issue are replete with problems. Thus whether children, depending on their age group, can understand the selling intent of commercials is a difficult question to resolve for the answer depends on such factors as whether open or closed ended questions are used.

Still, advertising does work and there is a significant correlation between television exposure and how frequently children request toys and cereals. A related factor is how often parents agree to their children's requests and strengthen this behavior. Research shows that parental acquiescence tends to increase with the age of their children.

Despite parental concern about the effect of television advertising on children's diets, study has found that while it does have an effect on children's nutritional status, this effect is very small and is likely to be harmful only to those children who are not well-nourished for other reasons, as children from families with small food budgets or with limited knowledge of nutrition. Factors of greatest significance to a child's nutrition are their parents' dietary education efforts and the family's meals, and educational programs could be targeted toward improving these.

Research has found that as children grow older they understand advertising better, but while their negative feelings toward television advertising markedly increases, there is only a slight decline in their responsiveness to commercials. This increasingly negative attitude toward commercials may derive from it being the accepted thing to criticize commercials, or apply mainly to the execution of commercials rather than to the products being advertised.

With each age level, heavy television viewers: pay more attention to commercials than light television viewers; place more trust in commercials than light viewers; have more favorable attitudes towards commercials than their peers; express stronger intention to buy products which are advertised on television.

The heavy, youngest viewers tend to be the most disappointed when the products are below their expectations, this decreasing by the 3rd grade as they gain more realistic expectations about products.

There is little evidence that either the clustering of commercials or their repetition affect children's tendencies to be persuaded by a commercial. The number of repetitions increases the remembrance of the name of the brand but not the desire for the product beyond one or two exposures. Adults frequently complain about repeated commercials but there has been no research on this point among children.

There are strict rules when advertising to children: that the product presentation is understandable and accurate; that there is no undue sales pressure as by suggesting that a child will be more popular by owning the product; that any required assembly is clearly stated; that endorsements not be made by program characters;

that the emphasis be on the product and not on the premium; and, most important of all, that the product be safe.

Younger children have the greatest difficulty in understanding the purpose of commercials which contain premium offers, believing that the premium is the primary product. Older children are much better able to distinguish the product from the premium offer though this depends on their level of cognitive development.

There are several general rules for effective television advertising with children: tell the truth, be humorous, and remember that kids want relief from stress and to have fun. Originality, good music which fits the commercial, and ads which grab their attention right away tend to be winners.

Most toy commercials use a life-action format whereas advertising for cereals relies heavily on animation. It is best to populate commercials with children who are about two years older than the ones you are trying to reach since anything babyish is the kiss of death. Children want to be cool which means being confident, respected, and always knowing the right thing to say.

With teenagers, having socially responsible themes and being politically correct are important. Though teenagers tend toward cynicism, they generally believe that advertising is useful for it helps them to decide what to buy. Teenagers care deeply about brands that match their image and personal needs and are loyal to brands that help them look good. They are trendsetters for younger children who look up to them to identify with, and from whom to learn the latest fashion.

Four family influences affect the consumer socialization of children: the goals which parents have for

Through Children's Minds

their child's consumer learning; the parents' behavior as consumers (their use of information and advertising in buying decisions); the parent-child interaction, as by not yielding to their child's purchase requests; and the child's opportunities for buying products independently (the child's income, the child's power to make decisions, the child's frequency of exposure to television commercials).

While adults don't generally talk about advertising since it is not something which they feel strongly about, a study found that most parents (73%) feel either strongly negative or negative about children's commercials but are willing to have such advertising in order to continue children's programming. Many (49%) had never seen any Saturday morning commercials and only 22% of mothers could cite a particular commercial which they felt was particularly bad for children.

Television advertised children's products were judged to be no better or worse a value than unadvertised products, and there was no apparent relationship between the degree of expressed dissatisfaction with commercials and parents' monitoring of their children's television viewing.

Since the 1970s the Federal Communications Commission has been concerned about whether children under the age of eight can distinguish between commercials and programs, and advocates separators between the two ("We will return after these messages."). But this ignores whether children are able to distinguish the separate motives of commercials and programs.

Research has shown that although children from kindergarten onward could identify the term "commercials," the younger children were confused about their concept and distinguished the commercial from the program on the basis of affect (commercials were funnier) or spontaneous reasoning (commercials were shorter than programs). Only do older children (9-12 years) understand the differing intent of both (programs try to entertain, commercials try to sell).

Children as young as four years could identify figures in commercials and match them with specific food products but were less able to make character-product associations when asked the more general question of which character was in a commercial. The difficulty which young children have in distinguishing commercial from program is reflected in the finding that younger children tend to pay equal attention to both as contrasted with older children.

A study found that the attention of preschool through 5th grade children was significantly higher when viewing clustered commercials than when these commercials were dispersed throughout a cartoon program; but no significant difference was found in either the children's recall of the commercials or expressed preference for advertised products.

Younger children try more than older children to influence their parents' purchasing but older children are more successful.

Most people consider watching television to be a passive activity and, in a sense, it is. The unmoving person peers at a screen image which changes rapidly. It is difficult to conceive of a more sedentary activity than this except reading. Yet television watching is, at best, just tolerated by parents while a child's reading is encouraged. One reason for this different attitude is logical: a child who cannot read well will have serious difficulty achieving in school and functioning in the adult world.

Yet there are similarities between reading and watching television though by using this comparison I do not declare that both are of equal value to a child's development. And I also feel compelled to state that research with adults has documented how unhealthy long periods of sitting is.

Most adults believe that to be active one must *do* something but this is not true. Holding a watchful attitude is also being active as is thinking, which is present in both reading and watching television. With both activities there is the psychological experience which video game creator's term *presence*, when the psychological world of the game substitutes for the real, external world and the player's involvement is complete.

Thus video game makers seek, as much as possible, to synchronize the game's sounds and physical experiences to retain *presence*, an experience which can be momentarily shattered by a parent's demand, as that their child's room be immediately cleaned.

The task of the marketer is to foster this experience of *presence* in their advertisement, to create a psychologically enveloping experience.

In earlier chapters I described how the cognitive abilities of children are far greater than most adults realize. From this derives an imperative: children are smarter than you think so don't try to deceive them.

And from the principle that play is fun comes the second rule when creating advertisements for children: let your imagination run free, and try to have fun yourself.

The third rule is to tell a compelling story containing one or more striking characters. Perhaps 18th century look-alike pirates sailing a branded-ship who rescue a family. The pirate-rescuers have been wandering for centuries, but seeking treasure not friends. However, this is a nearly impossible goal because of their fearsome appearance, which children can see-through but adults have difficulty doing. The attractiveness of such a commercial is that making friends is a topic of great interest to all children.

The commercial's story should, of course, be simple because of the brevity of a commercial. A series of gripping events, though rarely done, might be welcomed by child viewers. But the main point of the commercial should be clear since children are easily distracted by mounds of information.

Among very young children (1-4 years), active movement, animation, letters and script, reverse motion, and visual changes increase attention. Among auditory characteristics, attention is increased by lively music, singing, rhyming, sound effects, and auditory changes in general. But the use of other special effects (pixilation or slow or fast motion) doesn't change attention greatly.

Children's attention increases with the auditory complexity of a commercial regardless of its visual complexity. Thus, variations in the audio of commercials have a greater effect on children's attention than variations in the visual complexity. Hearing information is more influential than seeing it in print.

It is crucial that the wording in the disclaimer be appropriate to the child's age. Young children more readily shift their belief about a product than older children, and this indicates the need for even greater caution in advertising to the youngest audience.

The best ads have only two to three adjectives to remember and for children these generally involve having fun and being part of a group. Children like characters that they can identify with; those who are charming and having fun are always good. But they also should be figures who won't behave so skillfully that a child would feel, "I could never do *that*!"

The figure should have good taste as by not making fun of others though putting something over on an adult,

Through Children's Minds

as through having special knowledge, is acceptable since children and teenagers view themselves as inhabiting a different universe than adults.

When creating ads, the marketer must always keep in mind the age of their audience. While a teenager can readily pick out the most important idea, a younger child needs more direction and a slower pace. Because a young child can deftly operate a game on a tablet does not mean that they possess an adult's capacity for thinking, to paraphrase Jean Piaget's dictum about the difference between child and adult thinking.

Children don't like being called "children" and they particularly resent being called "babies." Pairing a child of the age of your target audience with an older child would increase the comfort of your viewers.

While teenagers want to see something with more sophisticated adult humor, the same program can appeal to both children and teenagers with the children enjoying the slapstick while the teenagers grasp the parody.

When dealing with a serious topic like date rape, while an adult might prefer a video about how the girl's parents helped her to fight the system, the teenager would prefer to see more about the girl's actions and the peer pressure she felt and the boy-rapist's reactions.

Children are used to a lot of action and color and the level of activity which would annoy adults produces a favorable reaction from a younger crowd. So it is OK to repeat the brand or information but do so in different ways since children appreciate novelty.

What is essential to keep in mind is that an advertisement intended for children is created for viewers with different concerns than adults. The task of an adult is to function in an adult world but the daily social battlefield which the child or teenager confronts is far different though containing equally great stress.

Through Children's Minds

Youth like to watch commercials and programs in which they are accepted as a separate group but also having concerns which are as valid as those of adults. And while they want to view themselves as being in control, they also know that they could not survive without the loving care of their parents. But this is not something which they want to be reminded of.

To summarize how children relate to television commercials. Repetition is important, and advertisements are more effective when they do not arouse strong emotions. Advertising does not arouse deep involvement in children, is not a topic of great importance to them, and does not produce in children any deep concern for "selling motives."

Effective advertisements reinforce accepted styles of behavior and never challenge them. The level at which advertisements make their effect is more subtle than the level of paying close attention. Children, when they put their minds to it, are aware of how commercials work but they do not wish to be reminded of this and advertisements which are obvious are the most disliked.

Commercials are, to children, a natural part of television, not to be sought out but to be accepted, and some are clearly remembered.

Every parent recognizes the importance of their child. For this reason the marketer of children's products must always keep the potential reaction of parents in mind. Every child is someone's child and their parent will quickly protest if they feel that their child is being harmed.

So while children may enjoy viewing the sight of parents being deceived by children, this should only be dramatized playfully and in a manner which adults would appreciate. Moreover, you should never lie to children by implying that a product will grant them greater abilities or social success. Fun is what children are looking for and this is something which no parent would reasonably object to. Unlike the statement that a product costs "only" a certain amount of money which implies that a parent who is unwilling to purchase it should be considered cheap or insufficiently loving.

Moreover, a product's performance should be obtainable by a child and not require adult knowledge or special tools to achieve. And be sure that whatever is shown is done safely and using proper protective equipment if necessary (though they should not be needed with children's products). I am continually amazed at how many adult home repair shows have demonstrators who fail to wear essential eye and hearing protectors.

Further important points are that a television commercial should follow its ABCD's: deciding on the target Audience in terms of age, sex, and lifestyle; describing the Benefit(s) which the product will offer the viewer; giving Consistent messages to both the viewer and their parents; and Deciding on a simple but exciting story. By following these rules, no marketing campaign will go far wrong.

The objections made by public interest groups about advertising to children are: that advertising to children is morally wrong, unethical, and distasteful; and that it exerts great influence on children who lack the sophistication to objectively evaluate commercial messages.

While matters of ethics and morality reflect personal values and opinions and not psychology, research has shown that children, except for the youngest, relate to advertising with greater sophistication than is generally realized, and that trying to fool them is a bad business technique indeed.

Through Children's Minds

The counter-argument by marketers is that advertising provides consumer socialization experience. That, through discussion with parents about products and experiences with actual purchases, children learn to make better choices as a consumer and gain a sense of responsibility, these being essential to their maturation.

The best defense against criticism about advertising to children would be research on such consumer learning processes as: the relationship between the parents' financial practices and those of their children; what parents tell their children about advertising, or do children learn more about it from their peers; how parents relate to their children's requests for advertised products as compared with other types of requests; how children learn about the uses of money and does this relate to intelligence and personality factors.

To very briefly summarize how children relate to television advertising: children understand most commercials, select the products that are interesting and attractive, and ask for them. This is little different from how adults relate to commercials too.

Chapter 18

Is Television Advertising Still Critical In the Digital Age?

With the exploding sale of tablet and video game devices, some marketers may question whether television advertising is still relevant apart from advertising electronic products, in these days when even very young children have become "digital native." Recently, a two-year-old boy, playing *Minecraft* on his mother's Smart Phone, said to me, "I take your picture!"

The LeapPad tablets for children age four through seven were among the top ten toys for 2012 as ranked by dollar sales. Yet, even such toys as Mattel's Barbie Digital Makeover Mirror, which enables children to, virtually, try-on lipstick and eye-shadow, rely on television for their sale though the Apps will be purchasable by parents on their mobile device. A toy company marketing vice-president spoke of investing more heavily on television advertising to make their Apps a successful, long-term category.

Research has found that adults don't necessarily object to advertising which is aimed at children for such things as toys, cereal, and clothing during children's programming, possibly feeling that it's good training for adult life. And "saw it on television" is seen by parents as lending positive influence to the purchasing decision.

But parents do object to commercials that "sell" sex, such as PG-13 movies, and products with poor nutrition such as candy bars. The adults who object most to advertising during children's programming were over sixty and least likely to be raising children.

"Television viewing" is an imprecise term ranging from rapt attention to merely being in a room in which a television is playing. Yet television viewing by children *has* declined. A study in 2010 found that viewership by youth ten through eighteen had dropped by twenty-five minutes a day since 1999, this being the first time it occurred.

While there have been temporary drops among adult viewers in the past, it cannot be said whether, in view of the explosion of interest in other media, this decrease will continue or whether the same TV programs will now be downloaded and watched on tablets, giving the child greater control over their activity but the programs retaining their same audience. As yet, very few families have cut the cable TV hook-up, and national networks still offer a huge audience.

Cost may be a factor. An almost unlimited menu of children's films (as *Dora*, *Curious George*) are available via the less costly Netflix streaming than on cable television, and children prefer the social and creative aspects of virtual worlds like *Club Penguin* and *Roblox*. That Smart Phone games are simple, cheap, and entertaining is another factor.

Another change in viewing habit is the success of such online video networks as *Awareness TV*, whose shows were viewed one-hundred-and-twenty million times in its first year of operation. Google's *YouTube*'s viewers watch six billion hours each month and other technology companies, Amazon and Hulu, are developing their own web video platforms.

This transformation adds the ability to change the video viewing experience from its passivity through the addition of viewer comments and sharing. Perhaps, with cartoons, children could even vote on their desired video plot events and outcome. This occurrence, in nearly real-time, might cause a major increase in viewership and viewer engagement. The ability of web networks to target

Through Children's Minds

narrow demographic sectors make them particularly attractive to advertisers.

Yet whether a video is viewed on a television screen or a handheld device, whether it is created by a national network, a cable channel, or a web network, the same characteristics will determine its appeal to children. These relate to their age, have been described in previous chapters, and will be summarized below.

Before children attend school they prefer programs with animals, animated characters, and puppets in a story format with much laughter and slapstick action. Visual factors which increase their attention include: active movement, animation, letters and script, and reverse motion. Auditory factors which increase their attention include lively music, singing, rhyming, and auditory changes in general with variations in the auditory complexity having a greater effect on children's attention than variations in visual complexity.

Older children of six or seven prefer child oriented adventure and variety programs, cartoons, and game shows. Children of eight to eleven years also prefer these programs though movies become increasingly important. Children of this age pay only two seconds less visual attention per thirty second commercial than do three to seven year olds. By the time a child leaves elementary school their viewing interests are more similar to adults than to pre-school children.

While the liking for commercials declines significantly with age (from sixty-nine percent for the 1st grade to twenty-five percent for the 5th grade); as does the level of trust for all commercials (from sixty-five percent in the 1st grade to seven percent in the fifth grade), there is no significant decline with age in the effect of advertising on a child's desire for the advertised product.

Yielding to the child's request vary by product

category and increase with the age of the child. The products with which children hold the most influence are cereals, snacks, games, and toys, they having least influence on the purchase of such products as shampoo and pet food.

The most effective television commercials: use short messages; have continual repetition; have realistically executed fantasy with an emphasis on motion rather than static pictures or words; have scenes showing how reward and enjoyment result from using the product.

A study of children between age seven and thirteen revealed no significant difference in the recall of television commercials between boys and girls. More intelligent children remembered more commercial content and more insistently used this knowledge to influence their parents' purchase decisions.

Because of the dumbing down of advertising so that it is understandable by children at all levels of intelligence, it may be that some ads are so unstimulating and simple that they're likely to be ignored. No problems requiring solution are posed, and no reasoning or thinking is involved. This raises the question of whether ads which are intellectually challenging might not be more successful with particular populations.

Because children do not yet have adult cognitive capacities, they have a limited ability to evaluate information. Thus advertisers have a special responsibility to protect children from their own susceptibility.

Advertisers should not create unrealistic expectations for their products; and must recognize that what children learn from advertisements may affect their health and well-being. These guidelines are particularly important since, unlike adults, children generally believe in commercials they like though this belief decreases as they get older when their liking for commercials decreases.

Being "cool" is of paramount importance to teenagers and what they associate with being cool is quality and that the product is intended for people their age. No consumer of any age would dispute the importance of these characteristics.

It is difficult to say whether commercials have less behavioral impact on children as they grow older since one must distinguish between intended behavior and actual behavior. Commercials may instill the intention to purchase or the desire for an advertised product but the execution of these, in most cases, requires the child to make a request of their parents and this has nothing to do with the commercial. Parents tend to agree to more of a child's purchase requests as the child grows older.

Finally, producers should strive for what the creators of video games term *presence*: the total involvement of the viewer with their production, whether it is a commercial or a television series, through the use of audio, visual, and story elements.

What is *presence*? I am reminded of a teenager's grumble that while engaging in sex with her baseball loving boyfriend he suddenly left the bed, found the remote, and turned up the television's volume to better follow the game. *That program had presence!*

Through Children's Minds

Chapter 19

Promotional Activities With Children

Though promotions aimed at children can include samples, contests, coupons, clubs, and events, all have the same goal: to increase the sale of a product or positive feelings toward a brand by associating it with a popular event or star or licensed character. But a marketing activity can quickly backfire if it isn't considered desirable by the child *and* their parents, both of whom will have long memories. Parents carry no greater hot button issue than their children, and marketing ethics are more important than temporarily increased sales.

Fast food restaurants have long used promotions, combining a small toy with the purchase of a meal to encourage the child to influence the family's decision of where to eat. Pity the restaurant which runs out of that week's promoted toy before the child gets to the beginning of the line.

When McDonalds's introduced Teenie Beanie Babies, each tiny toy being ID-tagged with its name, birth date, and poem, some stores fielded up to thirty inquiries a day from parents on behalf of their children who became avid collectors. Collector clubs and websites arose, one boasting that it received five million hits a week. Even adults began collecting them to humanize their workplace, lingering at the shelves while trying to select just the right animal.

Parents travel from one to another store in a restaurant chain, seeking to appease the howls of their child, only to be offered an alternate toy or one which must be purchased separately. "It's bait and switch, toying with little kids in the most cynical way," a mother remarked. This negative experience will color her

Through Children's Minds

behavior as a customer, and maybe that of her child too.

Yet meeting the demand of young consumers is difficult for it requires forecasting what it will be in six months, this long lead time being demanded by the manufacturing of these cheap toys overseas to save money.

Restaurants have learned that premiums should be used like courting gifts: varying the offerings to keep the relationship fresh and not being predictable. The best premiums are those which are durable and offer value either for play or learning. But premiums should be timely too and trying to determine the popularity of next year's character for a premium isn't easy.

Premiums have a long history, going back a hundred years to Cracker Jack's offer of a prize. Their popularity caused marketers to realize that it takes more than advertising to win the allegiance of young customers.

The long held belief that girls like dolls, home furnishings, and clothing, and that boys prefer race cars, outer-space gear, and sports items is generally true. But both boys and girls between four and twelve like toy animals, books, musical instruments, and games, and girls are more likely to play with a masculine item than boys with a feminine item. Secret decoders, printers, animal toys, stickers, and puzzles have a universal appeal. But age does count and it can be difficult to devise a premium that will appeal to both a four-year-old and an eleven-year-old though both will like the same kind of cereal.

Children from four to seven like rhyming, silly riddles, jokes, fantasy characters, and outer space travel. They have a low reading ability and short attention span and the premium toy should have only one function which should be readily apparent. They recognize logos

Through Children's Minds

so putting the logo on a premium is a form of advertising. Safety is a major concern and the in-package premium can't contaminate the cereal or be small enough to be swallowed by a child.

Children from eight to eleven want to be challenged by games and will stick with a game or a puzzle for some time if they can make progress. They love to be scared and enjoy surprises and suspense which explains the popularity of the *Goosebumps* book series. Frito-Lay has placed little *Goosebumps* books in bags of Doritos while Taco Bell has given away *Goosebumps* toys.

Children also enjoy categorizing and collecting things like small cars. Premiums for children in this age range should have more than one function.

Research has found that mothers prefer educational premiums and premiums that can be used by several children or by the whole family. They did not like plastic toys, toys needing assembly, and easily broken toys, with children also objecting to the latter. Naturally enough, parents, being more sophisticated, tended to regard premiums as being of lower quality than did children.

When a premium is mentioned in a commercial, its presence can interfere with a child's ability to remember the brand name with older children being better able to distinguish relevant from irrelevant information. Attention is selective and the length of the presentation may have nothing to do with how much attention the child paid to it.

For a supermarket to provide free snacks or a bank to offer lollipops or a silver dollar at the opening of a child's account can arouse a favorable impression in the child's mind and create a lifelong customer. But even an adult brand which is not associated with children (as a manufacturer of farm machinery or snow blowers) can

Through Children's Minds

gain a favorable connection by associating it with a charity drive or a fun event. Providing a fun event for a child will always work though research may be needed to determine what this consists of.

Schools, which often object to commercial marketing believing that the three R's don't include retailing, can be provided a magazine containing safety tips for parents and coloring pages for preschoolers alongside ads for children's products. An advantage of this is that there is no need for demographic data to be provided.

Product samples can be given to home economics, health education, and gym teachers, with these efforts being most successful were the teachers to be asked in advance what products they want *and don't want*. A book to promote literacy, along with a juice product, might be welcomed.

A successful event will capitalize on what is hot or will be hot in a child's mind such as an animated movie figure for young children or a sports event for teenagers. A contribution to a favored charity or a reduction in the admission price to amusement parks for collected labels have been found to be attractive.

A school based educational program to encourage reading would win favor with both adults and children. But care should be taken that the educational element is favored over marketing. Children note every detail and their allegiance as long-term customers can be gained and lost. Ideally, this event should be done in a space which children feel is their own little world, a comfortable setting where they can move around and not be forced to be quiet. Perhaps a tent-like structure with bold pastel stripes.

While I often advise adults that bribing children won't change their behavior for long, there is no question

Through Children's Minds

that it can have short-term results. At one time or another, almost all parents have used the promise of a trip to the convenience store or fast food restaurant to gain their child's cooperation, for a favored drink or to add to their toy or stamp collectibles.

Clubs and premiums often go together. A child will be offered a premium (stickers, a small toy, a poster) for joining a club, its purpose being to gain a data base. Children's premiums can also be offered to parents to induce them to make a purchase or to patronize a store, much like adults at supermarkets are provided the opportunity to complete a set of dishes or earn points toward a free Thanksgiving turkey.

A contest, which by definition requires the use of a skill or set of skills, is even more enticing to children. By using their developing abilities they experience the intrinsic motivation which is present in all learning and may gain them a desired prize too, this increasing their loyalty to the brand whose name is prominently displayed.

H. J. Heinz sponsored a nationwide contest for children, inviting them to create new labels for some of its ketchup bottles. After Heinz placed ads in magazines asking, "Hey kids, wanna be famous?" and sent posters to art classes, two-thousands of which participated, sixty-thousand children sent in their work. A four-hundred-and-fifty thousand dollar grant was also made by Heinz to the National Endowment for the Arts to help support children's arts programs. To reduce criticism, the materials sent to the schools were packed with art facts and art history to provide educational content.

Dixie Company asked children to send in riddles to adorn Dixie Riddle Cups, Crayola has asked children under twelve to rename eight crayons after their personal heroes, and Curad has challenged children to design new patterns for Band-Aids.

Many companies have realized that, particularly with the growth of single-parent families and the increase in private label products, children take the task of choosing consumer products seriously and speak up about more than products which had been traditionally marketed to children such as cereals and snacks. Moreover, parents frequently ask their children what they want to eat and will not purchase food which they won't eat.

Prizes can be offered for gaining good grades or by helping others, these being goals to which no parent would object. But prizes for contest goals do hold risks. If the contest is poorly designed and the task is beyond the children's capacities which vary by age, participation will produce not joy but disappointment and humiliation and this will overlay the child's future associations with the brand.

A company must proceed cautiously since early negative impressions are hard to erase with children. If a marketing project doesn't impress them it will be ignored or worse, be considered "stupid" and quickly become the butt of schoolyard jokes.

No venue is more useful for marketing to children than a children's club for it provides continuity and a focus for all of a brand's products. Children are natural joiners and are attracted by clubs. These raise their stature by granting them a special identity and membership in a group, and most children already belong to a sports club or to a "Y".

But for a company to gain this appeal is costly since the club must have a large continuing membership which requires a long-term corporate commitment. Backing out of a club will disappoint the child and thus anger their parents, which is not something that any company wants.

Through Children's Minds

Moreover, creating an effective club concept is not easy since even pre-teen interests differ greatly from those of young children. What is important with children's clubs is to provide fun and quality gifts and products. A tie-in with a licensed character or a charity is valuable.

Before beginning a promotion it is important for the company to decide on its purpose, whether it is to increase sales or to create a favorable brand image. Yet these are adult goals while a child's concern is whether the activity is fun and holds a place in their life.

Another adult goal, and one which is no less important, is how the success of the campaign will be measured.

Through Children's Minds

Chapter 20

Marketing, Children's Orientating, and Conducting Market Research

Marketing to children begins with children and the better that they are understood, the better they will be communicated with. One thing that makes children hard to understand is that they don't seem so different from grownups. They talk to us using the same words. But though they answer our questions, their answers can have different meanings for them than for us.

A child may say that they like product A more than B, and B more than C, but when shown A with C they insist that C is their favorite. A child may deny that there had been talk about food in a commercial which they just saw, stating that the talk was about the brand's name which is a food product (here, the fault was in the structure of the commercial).

Children can, sleepily, watch a show but when asked if they liked it, state that they loved it and enthusiastically describe a character. This explains why a product that children consider great can die in the marketplace while a low-rated product becomes the hottest item of the year.

A lot of American businesses are run on the assumption that everyone (buyers and advertisers and manufacturers) see things the same way. Manufacturers make products they like, and advertisers create ads they find persuasive. When the market consists of adults, especially of adults that share the same culture and values as the manufacturers and marketers, the system works pretty well. With children it works less well for this belief doesn't hold.

Businesses have tried to get around this dilemma

Through Children's Minds

by selling to the trade at an industry fair and not directly to children, or by selling to parents though it is their children who use the product. They may try a shotgun approach, using many alternatives in advertising, product development, and marketing, hoping for a few winners to cover the cost of all their losers.

Some manufacturers buy a license, thinking that if they can't figure out what children want, they should get onto a licensed figure's bandwagon. But as soon as children confront the fact that some experiences with a character are good and others are not, the unified identify of the license is lost and its marketing value ends.

Yet these are not bad things to do since they are much better than running a business with the assumption that you know how children see things when you really don't. But if you accept the challenge of seeing things in new ways you will discover that children are intelligent, understandable, and as logical in their own way as any group of consumers.

Children move through life by following one orientation after another. They seldom make decisions in the classic sense of the term. Their involvement with the marketplace is characterized by their global way of approaching things. If they focus on a product, they will look at it and align their bodies with it, direct their movement towards it, make contact with and eat it if it is consumable (and, unfortunately, sometimes even if it isn't).

If a product is not the focus of their orientation, it does not exist to a child. This is why younger children will tend to like everything on a ratings inventory. Not because they like the interviewer but because they approach what they notice, they like what they notice, and they have been forced to notice all of the items in the interest inventory.

Through Children's Minds

Because children respond globally, they do not have separate response systems which they try to integrate. They don't distinguish knowing from feeling or liking from familiarity. And neither should you if you want their behavior to make sense. For most children most of the time, liking and knowing are part of their same global response.

Children do not look for features and settle on those products which have them. They focus on the things they know and not their properties. Advertisers should keep their focus on the objects too.

Marketing to children involves steering them, setting up sign-posts to get their attention, establishing recognition. There may be many pieces to your product's message: commercials, promotions, display packaging, and the product itself. But since children respond globally, they see all of these as being indistinguishable parts of the same whole and you should try to preserve that unity. The product should be central, not spoken of while being alongside other objects.

When comparing the performance of children of different ages we tend to think that the youngest children react in a manner which can be characterized as sensorimotor, that school children relate concretely, and that teenagers think abstractly. Marketers relate this way, feeling that they must create one kind of appeal for older children and another for younger ones. But psychologists know that when more advanced ways of thinking are gained, the earlier ways of thinking do not suddenly disappear.

A person's highest level of thinking will be invoked only when the conditions are right. Teenagers will think abstractly when they are considering a product which they consider important, is in a familiar category, and when they are undistracted and their lower, better rehearsed systems of thinking do not point them in an unequivocal direction. But children who lack the ability or inclination or background knowledge or situation to think abstractly will not think in an abstract manner, and a model of abstract decision-making won't account for their behavior.

Commercials can appeal to a child's level of understanding through definition, association, or proposition.

Defining a product asserts to a child that the product exists and is to be noticed. This is the most primitive psychological level at which advertising works and it is often the most effective with children. If a product is strongly defined through its display and packaging, children will orient toward it. To best define a product it should be shown and labeled consistently, related to a person-like character and be part of a fantasy adventure or humorous scene.

Association links the product to other things in a child's awareness: emotions, activities, products, or people. If the stimuli associated with the product are well liked, children are more likely to orient to the product in the future.

Proposition is an if/then pitch. If children get the product, then they will get something else they want and for children this is to have fun. Other things usually don't work since propositional appeals have limited effectiveness with children as every parent knows.

Propositional type advertising is the most vulnerable to issues of deception since it is deceitful to make false promises though when children can't use propositional logic to guide what they orient to, this may not matter. Children in the twelve to fourteen year age range are most vulnerable to false propositions since they have just learned to organize part of their life

Through Children's Minds

propositionally and aren't yet very good at it.

The notion of conducting consumer research with children has only developed over the past forty years. Previously, marketing of children's products was aimed at parents who paid for them. Moreover, it was believed, how can one get inside a child's mind?

Too often, eyes glaze when the issue of research is discussed. And some, as Steve Jobs, were famous for their dismissal of consumer research, insisting that they could sense what people would want—which was true. Except, as one mother explained to her son when he copied his famous father by eating with his elbows on the table, "Geniuses are allowed to behave differently and your father is a genius!" Genius, such as Jobs' possessed, is rare.

The purpose of all research is simple: to provide accurate information with which to guide behavior. Admittedly, not all research is worthy of the name and price does not insure quality. There is better and worse research and low quality research can be costly.

Doing market research with children is not easy. It is particularly difficult in the toy industry where one year's hit can be the following year's disaster, and the reason why a child likes or dislikes a toy is stated as "because" with children hating or liking something in an arbitrary, black/white fashion though some researchers love five point scales.

While parents can provide some information, this is often unreliable, perhaps being swayed by the parent's unspoken attitude that there is something unsavory about marketing to children though its purpose is not to manipulate children but to discover whether a product meets a child's needs and expectations.

Still, much of the knowledge which market researchers seek is already known by parents though their information tends to be more accurate with pre-school than older children: that children like snacks upon returning home from school; that they are social and like activities with peers; that they know what they want and feel that they can influence their parents towards the purchase of it; that children over the age of ten lose interest in playing with dolls and toy cars.

Other information, gained through research, is likely unknown by most parents. As that few children under eight can remember advertised brand names though the recognition of likeable characters, the imaginary persona or real-life famed figure for the brand, is far greater. Thus a child need not remember a brand name but only a picture which can be found on a box.

While the limited language ability and natural shyness of children make them more difficult to study than adults, the marketing questions for both groups are largely the same: their response to new products and advertising; and their buying and media habits. For children, we must add the degree to which they influence the purchases of their parents and others though this is difficult to assess. Parents do not like to admit the influence which children have over their behavior. Parents may also not be able to estimate it accurately since their assessment is based on past behavior.

Despite its mysterious aura, the essence of market research is simply to help the manufacturer better understand their customers by asking them questions and interpreting their answers. Basic, essential guidelines are that the research should focus on a particular problem, be well-organized, unbiased by preconceptions, and produce information from which decisions will follow. If not, the research is window-dressing and a waste of money.

Many companies sponsor children's research

which seems indirectly related to the desirability of their product and is, moreover, not easy to conduct since, with regard to food, some babies like everything. Gerber Baby Foods sponsors research into all aspects of child nutrition to gain an edge on its competitors. One interesting finding was that breast-fed babies are more readily accepting of solid food than formula-fed babies because breast milk changes flavor depending on what the mother has eaten. Babies like unexpected flavors and infants suck longer and harder if their mother's breast milk tastes of garlic.

But with baby food products the parent is crucial too for, as a Gerber CEO stated in a *Wall Street Journal* interview, "If you can't get it by mom, you can't get it to the baby."

Before going to the expense of conducting research, there should be investigation of whether the problem raised has already been answered through other studies so you're not re-inventing the wheel.

One should be wary of the potential dangers of all market research: improper screening or respondents who behave "professionally": poor physical facilities; studies which are rigged to prove a point; and cities which were chosen because of their recreation facilities and food rather than for their marketing relevance.

Those contracting for research should be sure that they receive all of the information needed to evaluate its quality. Was a detailed description of the research process provided including how the participants were recruited and screened? Without these facts, the validity of the findings and whether they should be acted upon cannot be known. Thus, it is not only what was done but how it was done that indicates the adequacy of the results.

There are different kinds of market research

studies. They can be observational, as when children are observed in a nursery school to see whether a child spontaneously plays with a toy and for how long. From this, conclusions can be drawn about the ease of play and safety issues.

Though observing and recording the behavior of children sounds insignificant, it is not. A child may be unable to explain why they like something but close observation of their interaction with it can tell a lot. Moreover, observational research is sometimes the only way to get information about the youngest consumers. Preschoolers who aren't reading and writing can't answer standard surveys, and infants and toddlers who can't talk have greater communication limitations. But valuable insights can be gained by watching children interact with products, and with their parents too for parent-child involvement is a central element during infancy.

Observational studies are generally cheaper than conducting experiments or questioning directly. And with so many other things on their mind, parents often pay little attention to the details of children's play or consumer behavior which are important to marketers, as how a child behaves in a store such as reaching for and comparing items.

Observations cannot usually be made in the home and there is an element of artificiality when these are carried out in the laboratory. This deficiency is also present in experiments since a child may relate differently with the product at home or when they are with friends.

In a controlled experiment, the effect of a particular variable, or factor, is studied, and the results are compared with the group in which the element remained unchanged. For example, a new video game is proposed for sale to children. Are children who play it

Through Children's Minds

more likely to behave aggressively? This game, which contains much violence, along with the gift of the latest model game player, could be provided to children and recordings kept of their future interaction with peers. Is there now greater conflict? Do the studied children garner more school suspensions or behave more defiantly at home?

This unlikely to be performed research suggests the difficulty of studying children and particularly certain matters. While the children would undoubtedly love their gifts, parents might have concern. And behaviors such as aggression are particularly complex, being effected by numerous social, psychological, and family factors.

Questionnaires are used to learn what people think, and with children the personal interview is most often used. Similar, less effective techniques are used with adults in which surveys are done by telephone and mail. Here too, the age of the subject adds difficulties.

When proposing to interview children, the parents should be sent a letter describing the purpose of the study, and that a parent or guardian must be present during the interview, with the assurance that the child's privacy and identity are protected. A corporate telephone number should be given to verify and double check the interviewer's credentials. Money incentives should be given, and perhaps the opportunity to participate in a sweepstakes drawing with far higher cash prizes to several winning children. The interviewer should arrive in the home with gifts for the child: comics, yo-yos that glow in the dark, great-shaped pencils, and the like.

The ability to establish rapport with and to skillfully question children is uncommon, particularly since children often tell adults what they think the adults want to hear rather than expressing their real feelings. A skillful interviewer understands and accepts that children naturally act silly and make noise. The interviewer should welcome spontaneous comments and not respond as did the interviewer who was intent on investigating why women colored their hair. When the respondent broke in and asked, "Do you *really* want to know why I color my hair?" she was told by the questioner, "No."

What the market researcher seeks is to understand the *soul* of the product, the emotions and partiality of the customer. What is the boundary of the product? When is it used and with whom? What does it symbolize and what is the context of its use? Is the juice drank only at breakfast with a parent looking on, as part of a daily ritual, or with friends while watching TV or playing video games?

Focus groups are another useful research tool and some companies, like Nickelodeon, conduct hundreds of these a year. Here, a group of six to eight children is brought together for an hour or less to offer opinions about a product. These sessions are informally led by a moderator who, while structuring the discussion with particular questions, dresses informally and can relate with humor, not like the participants were adults by insisting that they sit around a conference table and behave "seriously." Though not a panacea, focus groups can be useful in gaining fluency in children's "consumer language."

One difficulty in conducting focus groups is that of maintaining a comfortable, friendly atmosphere. Other problems are that if the moderator's knowledge of the product is limited, they won't be able to immediately attend to new information presented by a child; or if they don't recognize that a child's response is intended more to impress the adult than "real."

Some companies maintain panels of children for

ease in establishing focus groups and to keep track of what is currently popular with children, their preferred snacks and fashions and slang. While being convenient, panels have drawbacks in that, over time, children age out of them. There is also the danger of the children becoming fatigued and relating as experienced respondents and thus no longer providing accurate data. The dropout rate can be minimized by keeping in touch with the children and parents on a regular basis and giving free products.

Focus groups can also be used to gain ideas for new products, to suggest changes in older ones, and to advise about advertising and packaging. Here, the screening process for group participants is more difficult since not all children are articulate and inquisitive and can relate to an abstract task and think quickly. If the selection is inadequate there are likely to be short, insufficient responses or follow-the-leader group dynamics leading to unhelpful data and misleading interpretations. It is important not to accept a focus group's results as gospel and jump to manufacturing or marketing decisions.

Focus groups are not usually useful until a child is over six. With young children, those of six to seven, the groups should be of no more than four children and it would be best if they were friends who had played with each other. Age groups are broken down into two year segments (as 6-7, 7-8). It is important to tell children that it is OK to say that they don't like something for this differs from how their parents often tell them to behave.

Parents can snack and enjoy the camaraderie of other parents while waiting and, to facilitate participation by older children, contact with these parents could be maintained through helpful mailings and the gift of products.

Role playing ("pretend you are...") is sometimes

used to gain information despite its shortcomings: the artificiality of acting, and the tendency to exhibit behavior which is socially desirable rather than realistic.

Attitude scales are sometimes used with children of school age, to gain a crude estimate of like/preference as by choosing the number of smiley faces on a scale. A drawback with this method is that because children tend to respond globally, they will often like everything on a list, not because they actually liked all of them but because they were not making a decision in the classic (adult) sense of the word. Instead, they were relating holistically, orienting themselves toward the product and, for young children, liking and knowing are the same thing.

When using the picture drawing technique, a child may be asked to draw a picture of how they use a product or what they first noticed about a store. While figure drawings have been used for many years by some mental health clinicians for assessment, this technique has little validity. The examiner is, essentially, melding their unconscious onto that of the subject to gain dubious results.

I was recently told of an applicant who failed the police recruit entrance examination in a major American city because, when asked to draw on three separate pieces of paper the picture of a house and a tree and a person, the House-tree-person test (HTP), he drew all three on one sheet of paper.

The HTP is a projective personality test which has little support for its *validity* (measures what it is supposed to measure) or *reliability* (the findings can be repeated), these being the two critical elements of adequacy of any psychological test. Research has shown that the HTP may have some limited usefulness in assessing brain damage.

Through Children's Minds

In rejecting the examiner's instructions, was this police trainee applicant asserting his common sense and independence? Was he likely to disregard instructions upon becoming a police officer? Or was he communicating that he found the HTP task irrelevant to assessing his capacities? I don't know though obviously the examiner who failed him thought that he did.

What is important to recognize is that not every psychological test is a good one, that is, that it possesses good validity and reliability. Also, that researchers tend to like gadgets, and the more visually impressive they are the better, and fancy statistical techniques which are understandable only to them and which publicize their skill.

The more that researchers practice these techniques, the wider the gap between market research and management becomes though this may not lead to conflict. If the manager's major desire for the market research is not to gain data but for another reason, and the researcher feels the need to exalt their art, both can share a happy symbiotic relationship. Not all market research is good—or winds up being used.

Projective tests (as, the Rorschach test, the Thematic Apperception Test), in which a subject *projects* their thoughts and feelings onto ambiguous stimuli, are valuable in diagnosing emotional stability and conflicts but less valuable to the marketer. The desire to use projective techniques in market research studies with children reflects the discomfort which researchers experience when studying children, who *do* think differently than adults.

Children are shy with strangers and not all adults relate well to children. Those who do, who can retain adult objectivity while being "one of them," are valuable, and should be given major responsibility in interpreting the research findings.

Because it is impossible to study all children of a particular age, a representative sample is taken to include those of differing ethnicity and background.

Common terms used in market research are: the *mode,* which is the most frequent number; the *median,* which is the middle number, half of the responses being above it and half below; and the *mean,* which is the sum of all of the responses divided by their number.

There are other terms in the world of television numbers: r*ating,* which is the number of households tuned to a particular station divided by the number of households that own a television set; s*hare,* which is the number of households tuned to a particular station divided by the number of households with a television set turned on; and *HUT,* which is the number of households with a television set turned on divided by the number of households that own a set. These differences are subtle but important to the heads of programming and to advertisers.

There are other categorizations of market research: developmental, confirmatory, and evaluative.

Developmental research is exploratory in nature. It helps to identify options and uncovers important factors for further consideration: finding ways of expressing the basic and distinctive concepts behind a product; finding ways of relating that concept to important customer needs; identifying barriers to purchasing that can be addressed by advertising; finding alternative product concepts or alternative advertising strategies for conveying particular messages.

Commonly used tools include focus groups, unstructured interviews, and observational techniques. Developmental research is basically an attitude and mandates being open to seeing unexpected things.

Through Children's Minds

Confirmatory research is intended to show the soundness of options, as the relative attractiveness of alternative package designs or whether a previously untapped market segment is a viable target. The tools used are surveys, behavioral laboratory tests, and field experiments.

Confirmatory research serves as a last minute form of insurance to make sure that a major mistake is not about to be made. Since product managers do not like bad news about their creation, it is important that the research design allow for all possible options, good and bad news, with an equal chance of each showing up.

Evaluative research weighs the effectiveness of strategies after they have been implemented. Examples of evaluative research include brand recognition measures and customer satisfaction surveys. Evaluative research tells you how well a strategy is working, as whether the advertising enhances customer understanding of how the product is related to their needs, but not whether the best ad was chosen.

While the dividing line between these types of research is often unclear, it is important not to rely on just one type of research to satisfy several needs. It is essential when using research that trust exists between the research team and the product manager.

There are good reasons *not* to do market research. These are when the marketing information is sought not to make decisions but to gain power for empire building, or to gain visibility in the organization by providing the impression of being modern.

Other reasons not to conduct market research are: to justify an already made decision; to "prove" that the product will be a success; or to reduce anxiety, as when it is felt that research is needed to serve as a potential scapegoat, something to fall back on in case of failure

Through Children's Minds

though the manager will not let the research findings influence their decision.

But researchers have sensitive antennae and usually manage to come up with the findings that their clients want. Researchers are also easy to blame if a product goes unsold. Here, it is the act of gathering information and not the information itself that is the important thing.

Some advertising agencies conduct market research not from belief in its value but to sell their services by attempting to impress the client with the belief that the agency is so sophisticated that it can provide all that client requires.

Though understanding the minds of children is not easy, relying solely on adult perceptions to produce and market children's products is more costly and doomed to fail. Yet even with a successful product it is important, after going to market, to study children's perceptions of the product and its marketing to determine if changes are needed.

www.ingramcontent.com/pod-product-compliance
Lightning Source LLC
Chambersburg PA
CBHW021155160426
43194CB00007B/754